Welcoming the Christ Child
Family Readings for the Nativity Lent

Elissa Bjeletich

Welcoming the Christ Child
Family Readings for the Nativity Lent

Illustrated by Jelena Jeftić

Sebastian Press 2017

God Creates The World

In the beginning, God created heaven and earth. Darkness covered everything, and the Spirit of God was hovering over the waters. God said, "Let there be light!" and there was light! He called the light Day and the darkness Night, and that was the first day.

Then God created Heaven, and saw that it was good; and that was the second day.

Then God gathered the waters into seas, and let the dry land appear between them. God said, "Let the earth bring forth grasses and trees that bear fruit" and it was so. God saw that it was good; and that was the third day.

Then God said, "Let there be lights in the sky to divide day from night." It was so. Then God made the sun and the moon, and the stars also, and God saw that it was good; and that was the fourth day.

Then God said, "Let the waters bring forth living creatures, and let birds fly across the sky." It was so. God saw that it was good and He blessed them, saying, "Be fruitful and multiply, and fill the waters in the seas, and let birds multiply on earth." And that was the fifth day.

Then God said, "Let the earth bring forth the living creatures: those with four legs and the creeping things, and the wild animals of the earth." It was so. God saw that it was good.

Then God said, "Let Us make man in Our image, according to Our likeness. So God made man in the image of God;

male and female He made them. Then God blessed them; and God said to them, "Be fruitful and multiply; fill the earth and subdue it, and have dominion over the fish of the sea, over the birds of heaven, and over every living thing that moves on the earth." It was so. Then God saw everything He had made, and indeed, it was very good. So evening and morning were the sixth day.

Thus heaven and earth and all their adornment were finished. And on the seventh day God finished the works He made, and He rested. Then God blessed the seventh day and sanctified it, because that was the day of rest.

Questions:

Every single day, God sees that His creation is 'good'. Why does God want us to remember that everything He created was good? Which part of creation was VERY good? God did not create evil things; He wants us to know that everything started out good. He also teaches us that human beings are VERY good.

When God makes people (at creation), He says that they are very good. Are all people good? All of creation is inherently good – because God gives people free will, they may choose not to remain good, but they begin very good.

God made people "in Our image". Why does He say "Our" image instead of "My" image? God is speaking in the plural (more than one – "Our") because He is a community of three persons – the Father, the Son and the Holy Spirit. The Holy Trinity exists before all time – it always was, it is, and it ever shall be.

What does it mean to be made in God's image? How has God made you to be like Him? Because we are made in God's image, we are like Him in many wonderful ways: we are capable of great love and of goodness; we are creative and free. God gives us dominion over His creation, making us stewards of the earth.

Advanced Discussion Idea:

If we read very closely, we can see that God is the Holy Trinity, even before time is created. In the creation, first the Father speaks ("Let there be…"), and then the Word of God or the Son makes it happen (it was so) and then the Spirit moves, bringing life to the new creation. The Father, the Son and the Holy Spirit—one God—work together to produce all of creation out of nothing, in the vast empty darkness.

Scripture references:
Genesis 1 through 2:4

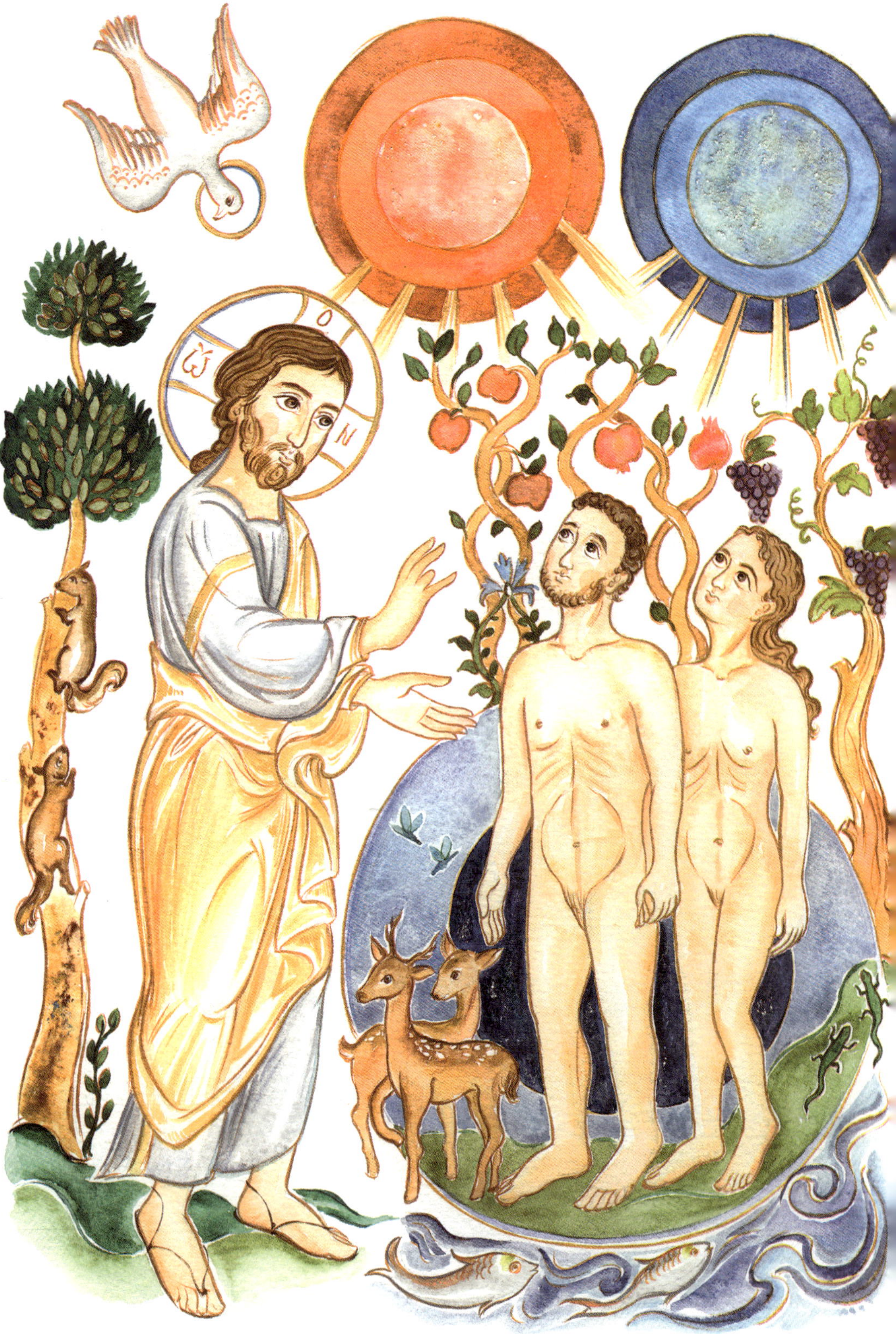

God Creates People

God formed man out of dust from the ground, and He breathed in his face the breath of life; and man became a living being.

Then the Lord God planted a garden in Eden, with every beautiful tree good for food to grow from the ground. Also, in the middle of the garden there were two trees: the tree of life and the tree of learning the knowledge of good and evil.

Then the Lord God took the man He formed and put him in the garden to tend and keep it, and He explained to him, "You may eat food from every tree in the garden; but from the tree of the knowledge of good and evil you may not eat; for in whatever day you eat from it, you shall die by death."

The Lord God said, "It is not good for man to be alone. I will make him a helper who is like him." God gave Adam the job of naming all of the animals of the field, and all the birds of heaven. But none of them was a helper who was really like Adam.

Then, while Adam was sleeping, God took one of his ribs and built it into a woman, and brought her to him. So Adam said, "This is now bone of my bones, and flesh of my flesh. She shall be called Woman, because she was taken out of Man." Finally, Adam had a helper who was like him!

Adam and Eve lived happily in the Garden God had created for them, never suffering or struggling. There was no hunger or pain, no sickness or death. In that perfect place, God was there with them, walking and talking with them.

Questions:

What was it like in the garden? Life in the garden was very pleasant. There was no suffering or struggle or fighting.

Why did God let Adam name all of the creatures? God gave Adam dominion over all of His creation. Adam was the caretaker of the Garden, so he had the honor of naming everything, but he also had the responsibility of watching over everything.

Why did Adam need a helper who was like him? Adam needs someone who is like him, made of the same flesh and bone, to be company and help for him in the Garden.

Advanced Discussion Idea:

Why would Adam need company? Because he is made in the image of God, and God is love; God is a community of three Persons (Father, Son and Holy Spirit) and Adam is created in God's image, so Adam is also created to be a part of a community of love.

How exactly did God make man? He formed him out of dust from the ground, and breathed life into him. St. Irenaeus compares this to the story of Christ healing the man born blind in John chapter 9: Jesus reminds us that He is the light of the world, and then He spat on the ground and made clay, then picked it up and anointed the eyes of the man with the clay – just as He formed man from clay.

Scripture references:
Genesis 2:4-25

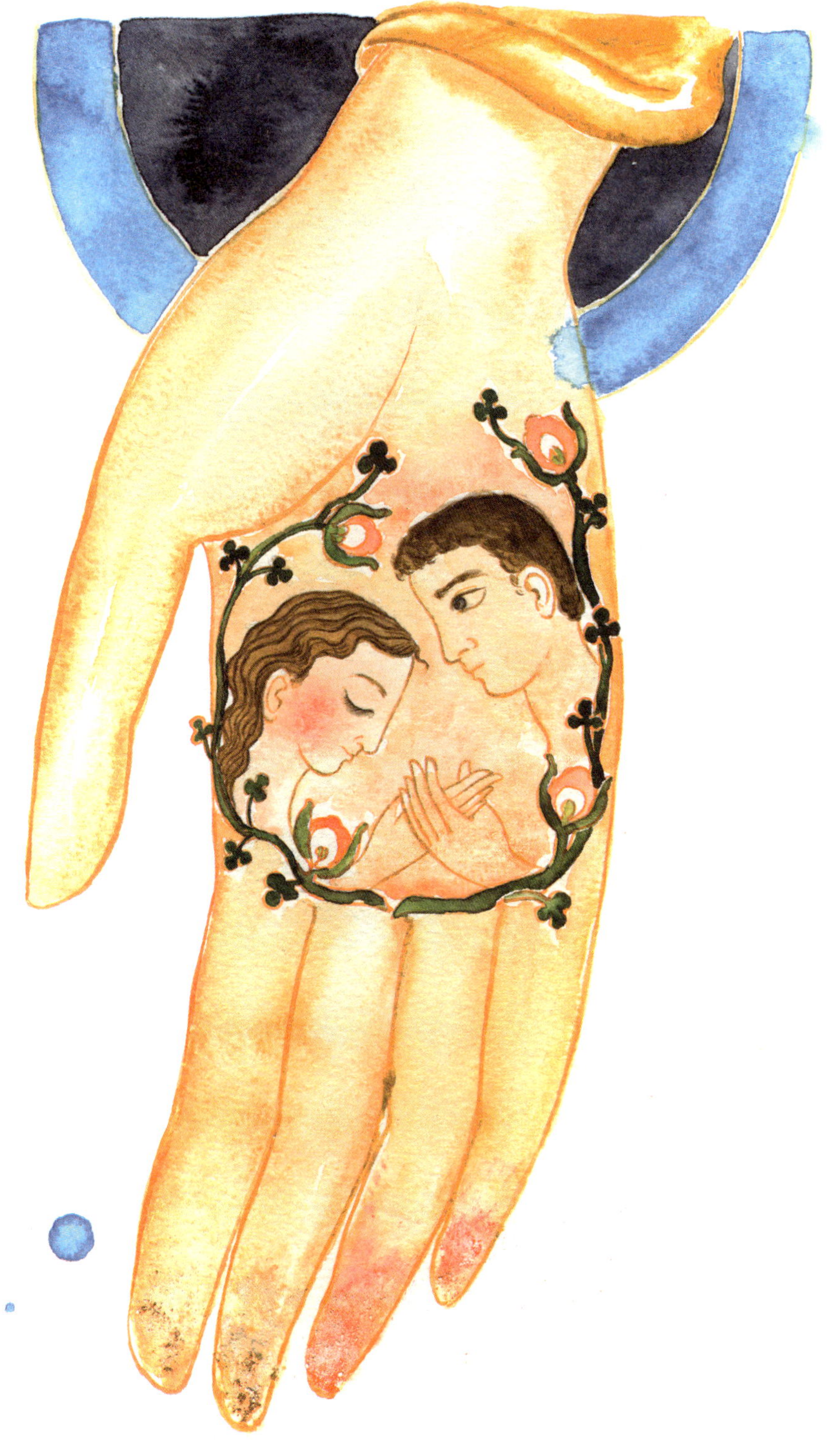

The Fall of Mankind

The serpent, the most cunning of all the wild animals the Lord God made on the earth, said to Eve, "Did God say, 'You shall not eat from every tree of the garden'?"

Eve answered, "We may eat the fruit from the trees of the garden; but from one tree in the middle of the garden, God said, 'You shall not eat from it, nor shall you touch it, lest you die.'"

Then the serpent said to Eve, "You will not die! God knows that if you eat that fruit, your eyes will be opened and you will be like gods, knowing good and evil."

So when the woman saw the tree looked very pleasant and beautiful, she took its fruit and ate. She also gave it to her husband, and he ate.

After they ate the fruit of the forbidden tree, they suddenly knew they were naked. They had never noticed it before, but now they felt ashamed. So they sewed some fig leaves together to cover themselves.

Then they heard the voice of the Lord God walking in the garden that afternoon, and Adam and his wife tried to hide.

God called out, "Adam, where are you?"

He replied, "I heard Your voice as You were walking in the garden, and I was afraid because I was naked; so I hid."

God said, "Who said you were naked? Have you eaten from the one tree from which I commanded you not to eat?"

Then Adam said, "The woman You gave me – she gave me fruit from the tree, and I ate."

So the Lord God said to the woman, "What is this you have done?"

The woman said, "The serpent tricked me, and I ate."

The Lord God said to the serpent, "Because you have done this, you are cursed! On your belly you shall go, and you shall eat dust all the days of your life. The woman's seed shall bruise your head, and you shall be on guard for His heel."

To the woman He said, "Now that you have done this, you shall bring forth children in pain."

Then to Adam He said, "Because you followed your wife and ate the fruit I told you not to eat, now the ground will be cursed. You will have to work very hard all the days of your life, sweating and toiling until you return to the ground from which you were taken. Earth you are, and to earth you shall return."

Then the Lord God said, "Behold, the man has become like one of Us, to know good and evil. Now, in case he also takes fruit from the tree of life, and eats it, and lives forever—" the Lord God sent him out of the garden.

God stationed the cherubim and the fiery sword which turns every way to guard the way to the tree of life.

Questions:

How did the serpent trick Eve? The serpent said that God was not telling the truth, and that He wanted to prevent them from being gods themselves.

Why did Adam and Eve eat the fruit of the tree of knowledge of good and evil? Eve chose to trust her own judgment over God's instructions; she liked the look of the tree and liked the idea of being like gods, so she ate it, and Adam followed her.

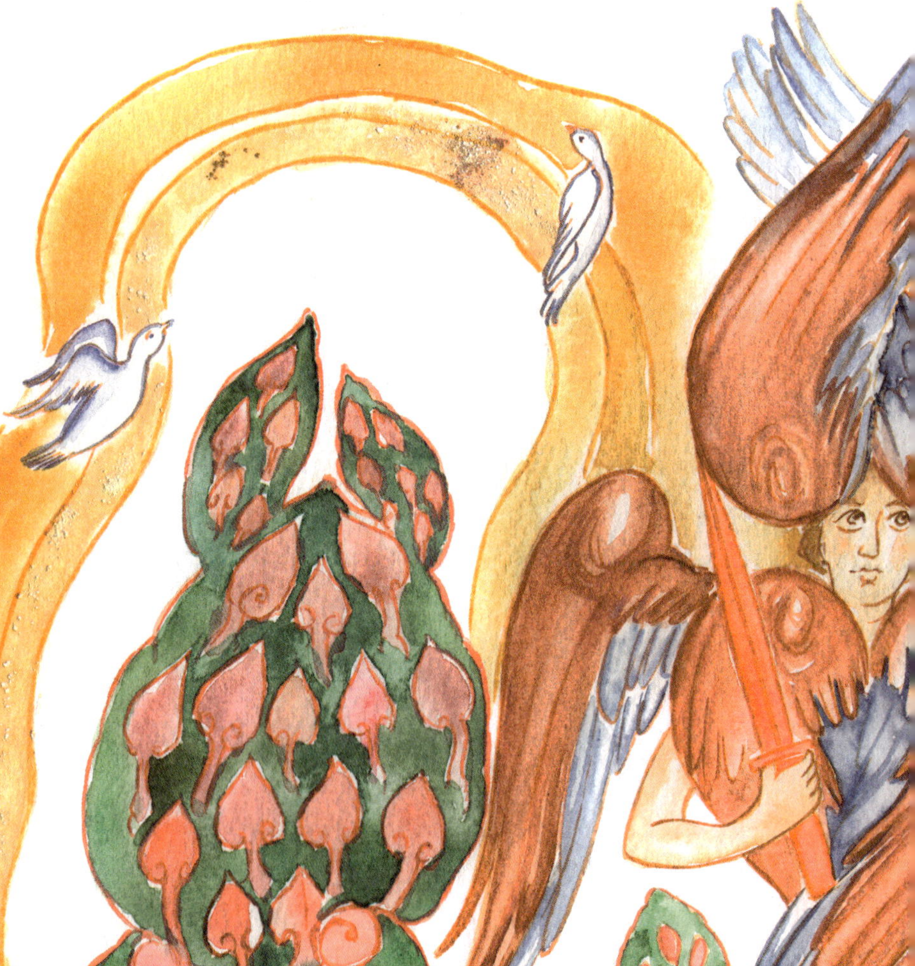

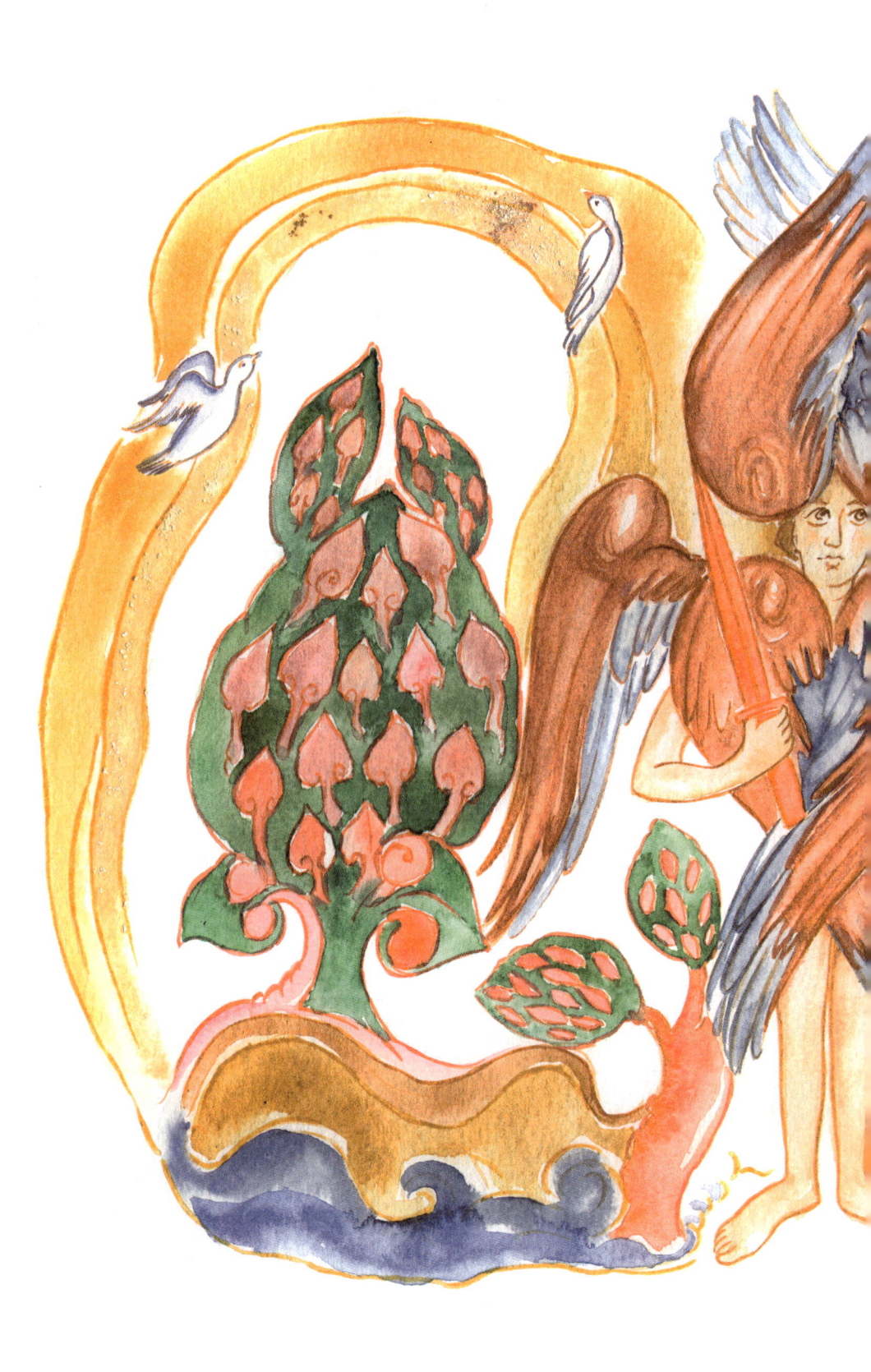

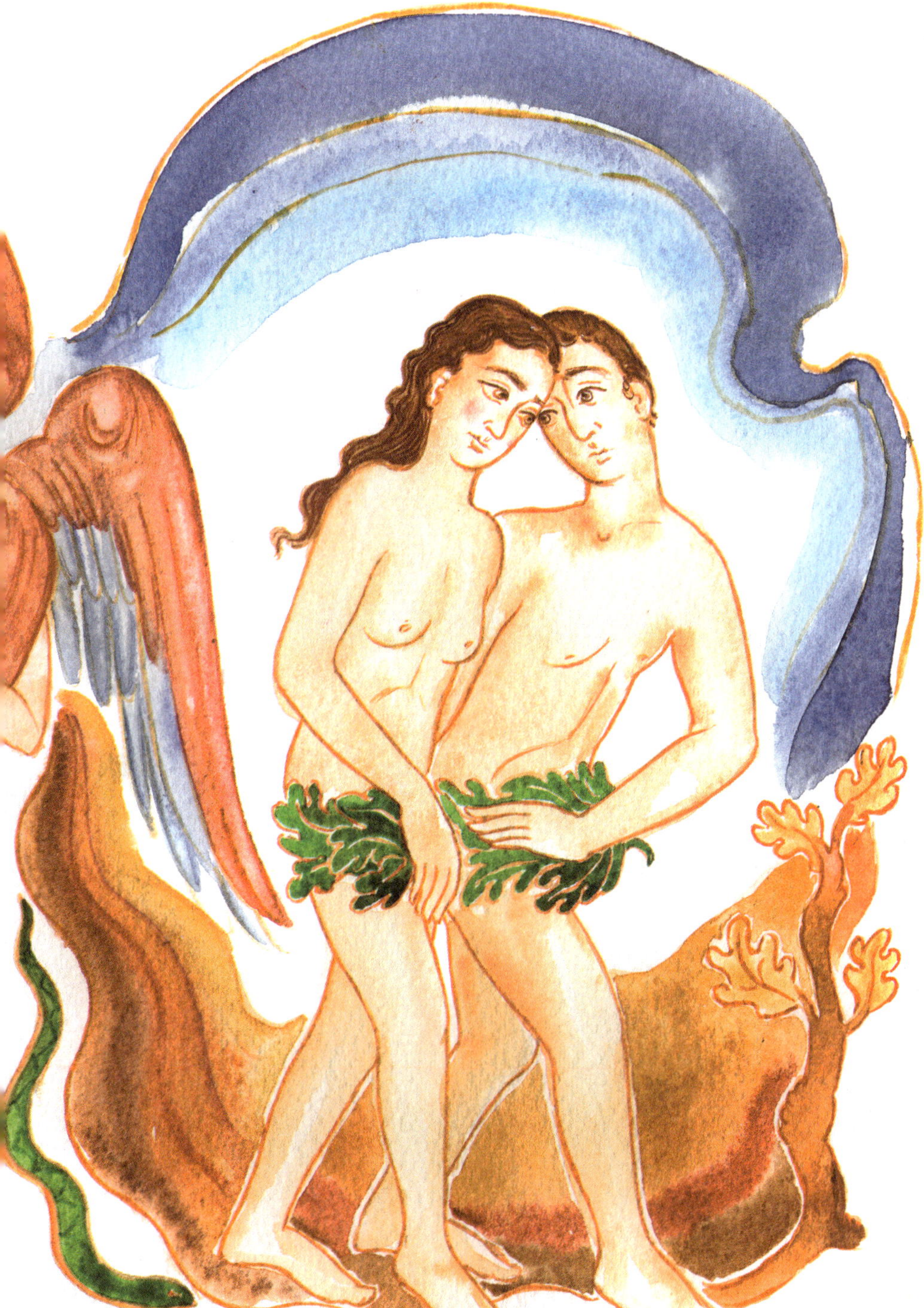

Was it really true that if Adam and Eve ate of that fruit, that they would know about good and evil? Was it true that they would die? Yes, it was true that they would know about good and evil like God does, and it was also true that they would no longer be immortal – before they ate the fruit they could not die, but now they would die someday.

Adam blamed Eve for giving him the fruit, and Eve blamed the serpent for tricking her. Who was really to blame for Adam and Eve eating that fruit? No one was forced to eat the fruit. Each of them chose to do it.

Why does God make them leave the garden, and why does He set up guards? Because Adam and Eve were not yet ready for this knowledge (though eventually they would have been), they were now in a miserable state. If God allowed them to eat from the tree of Life in their current state, their immaturity and misery would be permanent. Instead, God took pity on them and sent them out of the Garden, setting a flaming sword to guard the tree, so that they would mature and change before they ate of the tree of Life.

Who is the 'seed' of the woman that will crush the serpent's head? Jesus is the 'seed' of the woman (His mother is Mary, the "New Eve") who will crush the serpent's head when He dies on the Cross, tearing down the gates of Hades and defeating death by death.

Advanced Discussion Idea:
Adam had dominion over the animals and he named each one of them, but he did not eat them. In the Garden before

the Fall, Adam and Eve ate what we could now call a Lenten diet, and they lived in communion with God and conversed with Him comfortably. When they fasted, they were close to God. When they broke the fast, eating food which God had forbidden, their easy afternoons walking in the Garden with the Lord came to an end. How does fasting help us to overcome the difficulties that the Fall created in our lives?

Scripture references: *Genesis 3:1-24*

Noah's Ark

As the years passed, the number of people on the earth grew and grew. Because they were now fallen people in a fallen world, people were cruel to one another and their hearts closed down to God. They were so bad that every thought in their hearts was only evil, all the time.

God decided to remove this evil from the earth, to begin again with a clean start, when in all the world, God could find only one person whose heart was still good. That one person was Noah.

God said to Noah, "I will destroy the unrighteous and the earth. Make yourself an ark of square timber." God explained to Noah exactly how to build the ark – what materials he should use, how tall it should be and how wide. God explained exactly what the Ark would need to survive the terrible flood.

God told Noah to go into the ark with his wife and his son and their wives. He said to bring two of every kind of animal and every kind of bird into the ark; He told Noah how much food to bring for all of the people and all of the animals, so that he could take good care of everyone during the long flood.

Noah did everything exactly as the Lord God told him.

When they were safe in the ark, it began to rain. It rained for forty days and forty nights, and the waters rose and rose and lifted up the ark, and carried it high above the earth.

All the high mountains were completely covered, and the earth was under water. The waters covered everything for one hundred and fifty days. Then God made a wind to pass over the earth, and the rains stopped.

Very slowly, the water started to dry up, but it took a long time. Finally, Noah opened a window and let a dove fly out. The first time, she could not find anywhere dry to land, so she came back to Noah and the ark. But finally, Noah sent her out and the dove brought back an olive leaf, which meant that she had found a tree, and then the next time Noah let her out, she did not come back. She had finally found a dry piece of land, and a place to build a nest.

God told Noah, "Go out of the ark, you and your wife, and your sons and their wives with you. Also, bring out all of the animals and all of the birds, so they may increase and multiply on the earth." And Noah did.

Then Noah built an altar to God, and God said, "I will never again curse the earth because of man's works" and He sent a rainbow to seal His promise.

Questions:

Why did God decide to flood the earth? God flooded the earth because human beings had become so cruel that every single thought they had was evil. There was no good, and there was no appreciation of goodness, left in them.

What might have happened if Noah refused to build the ark? If Noah had not cooperated, the animals and people could not have been saved. God is powerful and can do things alone, but He likes to involve us – He gives us a job in His work.

What if Noah had not followed God's careful instructions and had built the ark in a different way? God gave very specific instructions to Noah, telling him exactly what he needed to know to be saved. If he had built the ark incorrectly, it might not have survived the very long flood, or held enough food to take care of everyone. We sometimes say that the Holy Church is like Noah's ark – it is built according to God's specific instructions so that we can be saved: He tells us to love one another, to fast and to pray, to receive the sacraments. We trust God and His Word, and God protects us inside our Holy Church from the storms outside.

Will God ever flood the earth again? God promised that He would never flood the earth again, no matter how bad people's hearts might be.

Advanced Discussion Idea:

Baptism is a washing away of evil and sin, just like the flood. God did not destroy His creation, but He washed away the evil that was in it. When we are baptized, we are also covered with water to wash away our sins, and then we finish with chrismation: the Holy Spirit is sealed inside of us with Chrism, which is a very special oil blessed by the Holy Spirit. Remember that the Holy Spirit appeared in the form of a dove when Jesus was baptized! Because the Great Flood is a foreshadowing of the mystery of baptism, it ends with the dove, holding an olive branch – it finishes with reminders of chrismation, and Noah builds an altar to thank God.

Scripture references:
Genesis, chapters 6 through 8

SAINT NOAH

The Hospitality of Abraham

*A*bram was a good man, and he loved God. So when God told him to pack up all of his possessions and to take his wife to a new land, Abram did.

When they arrived in the land of Canaan, the Lord appeared and said, "To you and your family after you, I will give this land." So Abram built an altar to the Lord.

The Lord said to him, "Look up at the sky, and try to count the stars. There are too many to count! Your children and your children's children will be like that. There will be too many to count. Your people will be nations."

Then God changed his name! He said, "You are no longer Abram, but now your name is Abraham. Also Sarai your wife is now named Sarah. And I will send her a new baby son, and I will bless him, and nations and kings of nations will come from him."

Then Abraham fell on his face and laughed, and said in his mind, "Shall we have a new baby, when I am one hundred years old, and Sarah is ninety years old?"

Then God said, "Yes, Sarah will have a son, and you shall name him Isaac."

Then one day, God visited them! Abraham was just sitting in the tent door at lunchtime and he looked up, and saw that three men were standing in front of him. He ran to them and bowed down to the ground, and said, "O Lord, please do not pass by Your servant. Let us bring water and let them wash Your feet, while You cool Yourselves under the tree. And I will bring bread for You to eat."

They said, "Do as you have said."

So Abraham hurried into the tent and he and Sarah prepared a wonderful meal for them. Abraham brought out the food, and set a table for them to eat.

Then God said to him, "Behold, Sarah is going to have a baby boy."

Sarah was listening in the tent door behind him, and she laughed quietly, thinking that she was too old to have a baby.

Then the Lord said to Abraham, "Why did Sarah laugh to herself, saying, 'How can I bear a child, since I am old?' Is anything impossible with God? At the appointed time I will return and Sarah shall have a son."

But Sarah was afraid and tried to pretend, saying, "I did not laugh"; but God said, "No, but you did laugh."

Questions:

What is Abram's "seed"? What does it mean to be a 'father of nations'? *Abraham's "seed" will be the people who come after him. He and Sarah will have a son, and then that son will have many children, and whole nations will grow from their family. That means that Abraham will be very important in the history of God's people. Sometimes people are famous for a little while, but then everyone forgets them. God has given Abraham a special job, to be the one who starts the important family that will lead God's people. In fact, Abraham's family will include many important kings, especially the most important one: Jesus Christ.*

Why does God change their names? *God gives Abram and Sarai new names (Abraham and Sarah) to signify a new beginning and new life.*

Why did they keep laughing at the idea of a new baby? Do 90- and 100-year olds have babies very often? Why would God send a baby to such a very old couple? When people are 90 or 100 years old, they don't usually have babies anymore. Human bodies are not fertile anymore when they get very old. God often chooses couples who are too old to have babies and sends them a wonderful baby, so that everyone will understand that this child is a miracle, a special gift from God.

Who were the three men who visited Abraham and Sarah? How did Abraham and Sarah treat them? *The three men who visit Abraham and Sarah are sometimes called angels, but Abraham calls them "Lord" because he understands that God is visiting him. When they speak, they speak as one. We understand that this is the Holy Trinity appearing as three persons: Father, Son and Holy Spirit.*

Advanced Discussion Idea:

Hospitality means showing love to visitors; it's making your guests feel at home. Abraham offers a wonderful example of this when he runs to serve his guests: he takes care of them himself, not merely sending servants but becoming their humble servant. St. Theodoros, said that "… Even if you have only bread or water, with these you can still meet the dues of hospitality. Even if you do not have these, but simply make the stranger welcome and offer him a word of encouragement, you will not be failing in hospitality. Think of the widow mentioned in the Gospel by our Lord: with two mites she surpassed the generous gifts of the wealthy." Are there opportunities in your own life where you might show hospitality? God is inside all of us and every person is an icon of Christ, so whenever you show hospitality, you will be serving God as Abraham did.

Scripture references: *Genesis 12:1-7; 15:1-6; 17:1-19; 18:1-15*

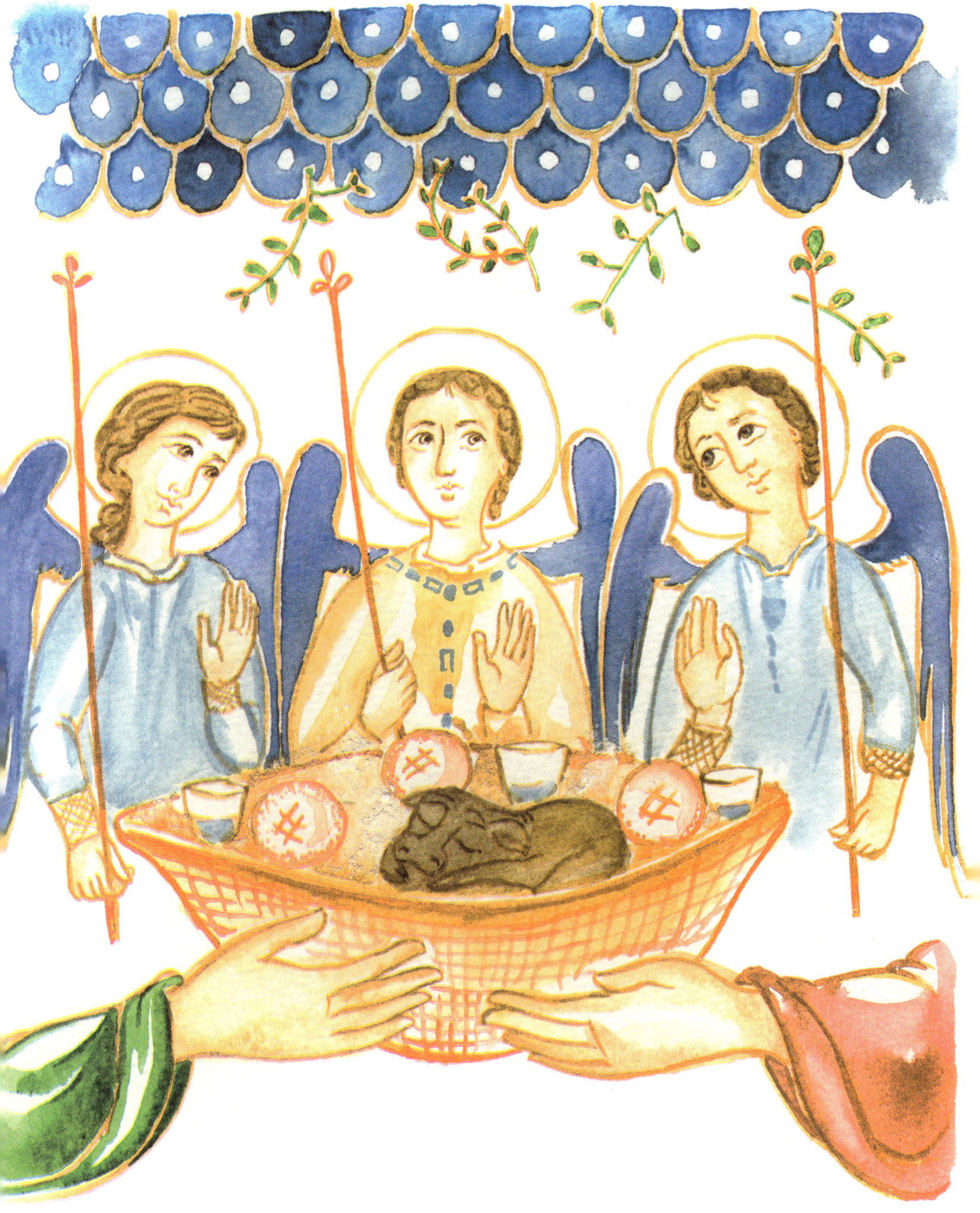

Jacob & Esau

Abraham and Sarah had a wonderful son, and they named him Isaac, meaning 'he laughed' just as God told them to do.

Isaac grew up and married Rebekah, and he prayed that the Lord would send them children, so God sent them twin boys. Rebekah could feel that they were wrestling and struggling with each other in her belly, and she asked God why. He answered, "Two nations are in your womb. One shall be stronger than the other, and the older shall serve the younger."

Now even though twins are exactly the same age, back then only the firstborn son had the 'birthright'; this meant that he would be the leader of the family after his father died, and he would inherit twice as much as his brothers. When Isaac and Rebekah's twins came, the red and furry little baby Esau was the first to be born and Jacob was born just behind him, with his hand holding onto Esau's heel.

As the boys grew, Esau became a skillful hunter. He was his father's favorite, because Isaac loved the meats he would bring home. On the other hand, Rebekah preferred her younger son, Jacob.

One day Jacob cooked a delicious stew, and when Esau came home tired from working in the field, he asked Jacob, "Let me taste this red stew, for I am exhausted." But Jacob looked at him and said, "Sell me your birthright today." Esau replied, "Look, I am about to die of hunger. What good then is this birthright to me?" So Jacob said, "Swear to me today." and Esau swore to him, and sold his birthright to Jacob.

When Isaac was old and his eyes were so dim that he could not see, he called his oldest son Esau and said, "Behold now, I am old. I do not know the day of my death. Please take your bow, and go out to the field and hunt for me and bring me some delicious food, that I may eat and may bless you before I die."

Isaac's wife, the boys' mother Rebekah, was listening and she knew that Isaac was going to give Esau the special blessing. While Esau was out hunting, Rebekah told her younger son about the blessing. She told Jacob to go quickly and bring some very good sheep so that she could make his father some food that he would love, and then Jacob could bring it to his father and receive his blessing before his death.

Jacob was worried. He said to his mother, "Look, Esau my brother is a hairy man, and I am a smooth-skinned man. Perhaps my father will feel me and know that I am tricking him; and I shall bring a curse on myself and not a blessing."

But his mother insisted, saying that the curse would be on her and not on Jacob. So they prepared the sheep and then Rebekah dressed Jacob in Esau's clothes and put animal skins on his hands and neck.

Jacob went to his father and said, "My father. I am Esau your firstborn; I have done just as you told me; arise, sit and eat, that your soul may bless me." Then Isaac said to Jacob, "Come near, that I may feel you, my son, whether you are my son Esau or not." So Jacob went near to Isaac his father, and he felt him and said, "The voice is Jacob's, but the hands are Esau's." But because his hands were hairy like Esau's, he said, "Are you my son Esau?" Jacob said, "I am." And Isaac gave him the blessing of the firstborn, making his brothers his servants.

Now it happened, just a few moments later, Esau came in from hunting. He also had made savory food, and brought it to his father, and said, "Let my father arise and eat of his son's game, that your soul may bless me." And his father Isaac said to him, "Who are you?" So he said, "I am your son, your firstborn, Esau." Then Isaac trembled, and said, "Who? Where is the one who hunted game and brought it to me? I ate all of it before you came, and I have blessed him—and indeed, he shall be blessed."

When Esau heard the words of his father, he cried with an exceedingly great and bitter cry, and said to his father, "Bless me—me also, O my father!" But he said, "Your brother came with deceit and has taken away your blessing." Then Esau said, "Jacob took away my birthright, and now look, he has taken away my blessing."

Questions:

Why did Esau lose his birthright to Jacob? Esau was hungry and tired, so he traded his birthright for a bowl of stew.

Which is more valuable: a birthright or a bowl of stew? What does this tell us about Esau? Esau must not have cared much for his birthright, and was impulsive. He valued immediate gratification (food in his belly right now) over long-term value (inheriting all of his father's lands and possessions and becoming the leader of the family).

Why would Rebekah help her younger son trick Isaac as he was dying? Rebekah remembered God's words, that her sons were like 'two nations' struggling with each other, and that the younger would rule over the elder. She also knew that Esau had already traded his birthright for a bowl of stew, and she preferred Jacob to Esau.

Advanced Discussion Idea:

When we talk about this particular birthright and blessing, we must remember that this is Abraham's seed. God promised Abraham that he would father nations, and that kings would come from his line. The brother with the birthright will lead this very important family which will father nations and kings of nations. When Jacob receives the birthright and the blessing, he becomes the patriarch of a family line which God promises will bless the entire world. How? It will produce the King of Kings, Jesus Christ, who will deliver us from death.

Scripture references: Genesis 25:21-33 and 27:1-40

Jacob's Ladder

Esau hated Jacob for taking his blessing, and he said in his mind, "Let the days of mourning for my father draw near, then I will kill my brother Jacob." But their mother, Rebekah, heard about it, and told Jacob to go back to her homeland and stay with brother, Laban, until Esau calmed down.

Isaac agreed, and he called Jacob and blessed him, and said, "Go to the land of your mother and her family, and find a wife there. May God bless you and give you the blessing of Abraham, to you and your seed, so that you may inherit the land which God gave to Abraham."

So Jacob journeyed to the land where his uncle lived. Along the way, he stopped to camp for the night, and he lay down to sleep with a stone under his head. Then he dreamed that a ladder was set up on the earth, and its top reached to heaven; and there the angels of God were going up and down the ladder.

The Lord stood above the ladder and said, "I am the Lord God of Abraham your father, and the God of Isaac. Do not fear, this land I will give to you and your seed. In you and in your seed, all the tribes of the earth shall be blessed. Behold, I am with you."

Then Jacob awoke from his sleep and said, "The Lord is in this place, and I did not know it. How awesome is this place! This is none other than the house of God, and this is the gate of heaven."

Questions:

Why was Jacob traveling to the land of his mother and her family? Esau was very angry with Jacob and was thinking of killing him, so Jacob left to keep safe from Esau. In addition,

Isaac felt that it would be best if he found a wife there, in his mother's homeland.

What does it mean that Isaac gave his son, Jacob, the blessing of his father Abraham? Isaac continues to give blessings to his son, Jacob, even without the trickery that happened earlier. Truly, Isaac loves his son, and Jacob has the birthright and blessing of Abraham. Even God will say that Jacob really has the blessing of Abraham during the ladder dream.

Where does the ladder go, and who is climbing it? The ladder goes from earth to heaven, and the angels go up and down.

Advanced Discussion Idea:

Jacob dreams of a ladder that goes up to heaven, with our Lord Jesus Christ standing at the top, welcoming him and offering him great blessings. The ladder is a wonderful way to think about the effort required of a Christian: it's not an easy jump up to heaven, but it's a path that requires climbing. Through effort, through prayer and fasting, the Christian slowly climbs the ladder to higher levels of spiritual development. As St. John Climacus said, "no one can climb a ladder in one stride" (or step).

In addition, the beautiful hymns of the Church teach that the the ladder is like the Theotokos: just as the ladder provides a pathway between heaven and earth, the Theotokos is the way that God comes down to our level. By giving birth to God in the flesh, the Theotokos has become the bridge, the ladder, between heaven and earth.

Hail, heavenly ladder, by whom God came down!
Hail, bridge leading earthly ones to heaven!
—Akathist Hymn to the Theotokos

Scripture references: *Genesis 27:41-28:22*

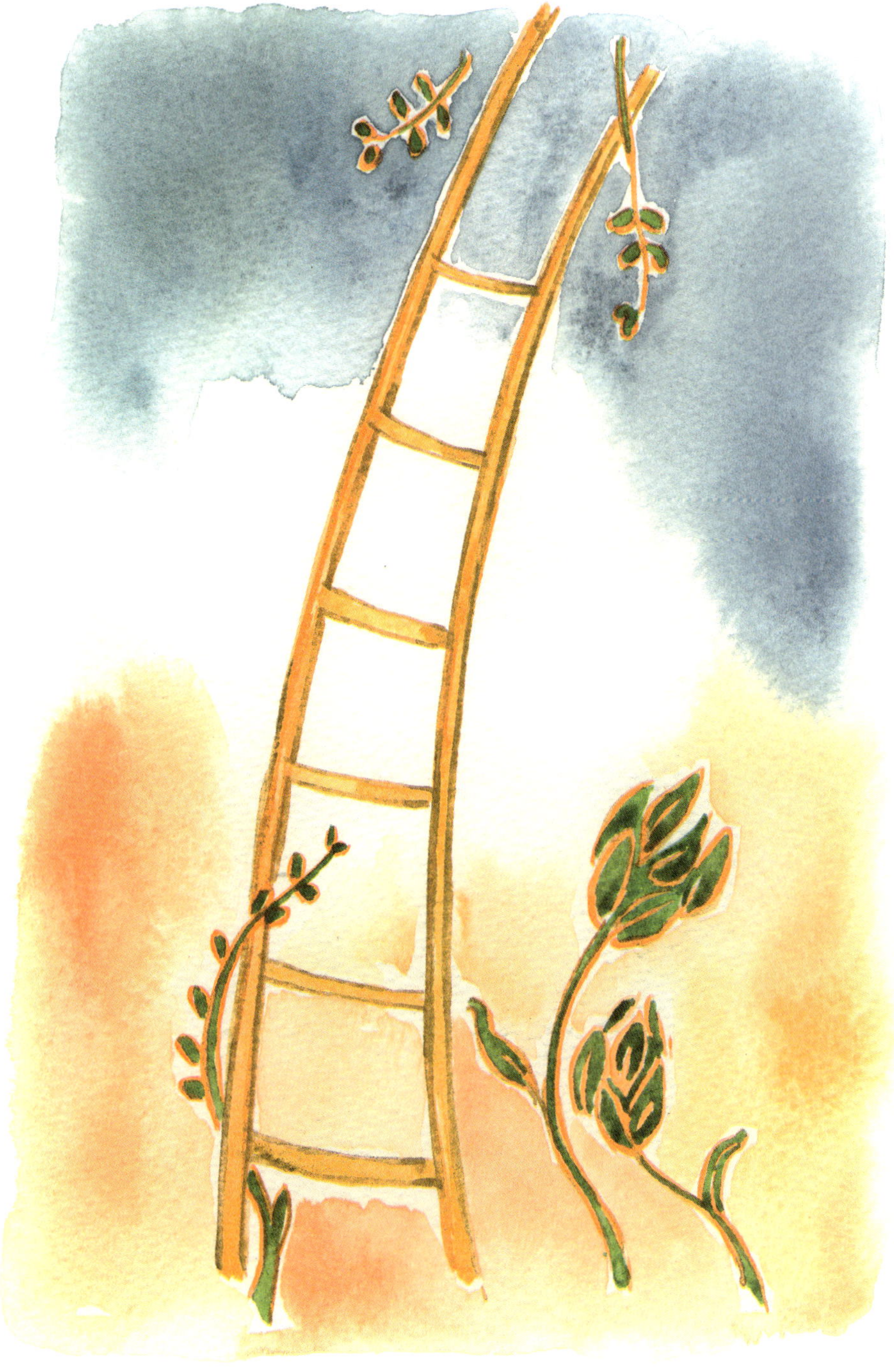

Joseph & the Coat of Many Colors

*J*acob had twelve sons, but he loved the youngest one, Joseph, the most. He showed his love by making him a very beautiful coat of many colors, and when his brothers saw it, they were angry. They knew that their father loved Joseph more than he loved them.

Just as God sent his father, Jacob, a dream vision of the ladder, God sent Joseph meaningful dreams too. Sometimes, those dreams seemed too proud, and his family didn't like them.

One day, he told his brothers that, in his dream, they were all tying wheat into nice bunches, and then suddenly Joseph's wheat rose up and all of his brothers' wheat bowed down to Joseph's wheat. So his brothers said to him, "Are you hoping to be king over us?" and they hated him even more. Then he dreamt that the sun and the moon and eleven beautiful stars all bowed down to him – meaning that his dad and his mom and his eleven brothers would all bow down to him someday. His brothers grew more and more envious and angry with him.

One day, Joseph's brothers were tending sheep, and when they saw him walking toward them, they decided to kill him and throw him into a pit; they planned to lie to their father, and pretend that a wild beast had eaten him.

But one of the brothers said no. Reuben said that they shouldn't kill him; he suggested that they just throw him into a pit instead, because secretly he planned to go back and rescue Joseph, so that he could return him safely to their father.

So when Joseph came to his brothers, they stripped the coat of many colors off him. Then they threw him into a deep, empty pit and then, as if nothing at all was wrong, they sat down to eat a nice meal. Off in the distance, they noticed some people coming along the road, riding on camels and bringing spices, balm, and myrrh. They were traders, headed to Egypt.

So Judah said, "Joseph is our brother – let's not kill him or hurt him. We can just sell him to these traders instead." The brothers agreed, and they pulled Joseph out of the pit and they sold him for twenty pieces of gold. The traders took Joseph to Egypt.

When Reuben returned and saw that Joseph was not in the pit, he was very upsct.

The brothers needed a story to tell their father, so they killed a young goat and dipped Joseph's coat of many colors in the blood. Then they brought it to their father and pretended that a wild animal had taken Joseph away from them. Jacob was terribly sad to have lost his favorite son. All his sons and daughters tried to comfort him but he could not be comforted.

Questions:

What did the dreams that God sent to Joseph mean? God sent Joseph dreams about how he would hold a place of honor, and his brothers and even his parents would bow down to him, showing him respect. This was a prediction from God, a vision of the future.

Why were Joseph's brothers so angry with him? They were angry with Joseph because they were jealous that his father loved him more and that God was sending visions of how important he would be. Because Joseph was the youngest brother, his older brothers were especially annoyed at the idea that they would bow to him – after all, as the youngest, he should be bowing to them.

What was Rueben's plan and why didn't it work? Reuben did not think it was right to kill their own brother, so he was secretly planning to rescue Joseph and take him back, alive and well, to his father. Unfortunately, while he was gone, his brothers sold Joseph to the traders, so he couldn't bring him to Jacob.

Advanced Discussion Idea:

The Church Fathers describe Joseph as being, in many ways, like Jesus. He didn't do anything wrong, but other people envied him. They didn't really understand the prophecies about his future, so they worried that he would be more powerful than them and attacked him to preserve their own earthly power. Both of them were betrayed for a small amount of money: Jesus for 30 pieces of silver, and Joseph for 20 pieces of gold. Both went into a pit – Joseph was thrown in the dark pit until the slave traders came, and Jesus was in the dark pit of Hades after His crucifixion.

Scripture references: *Genesis 37: 3-35*

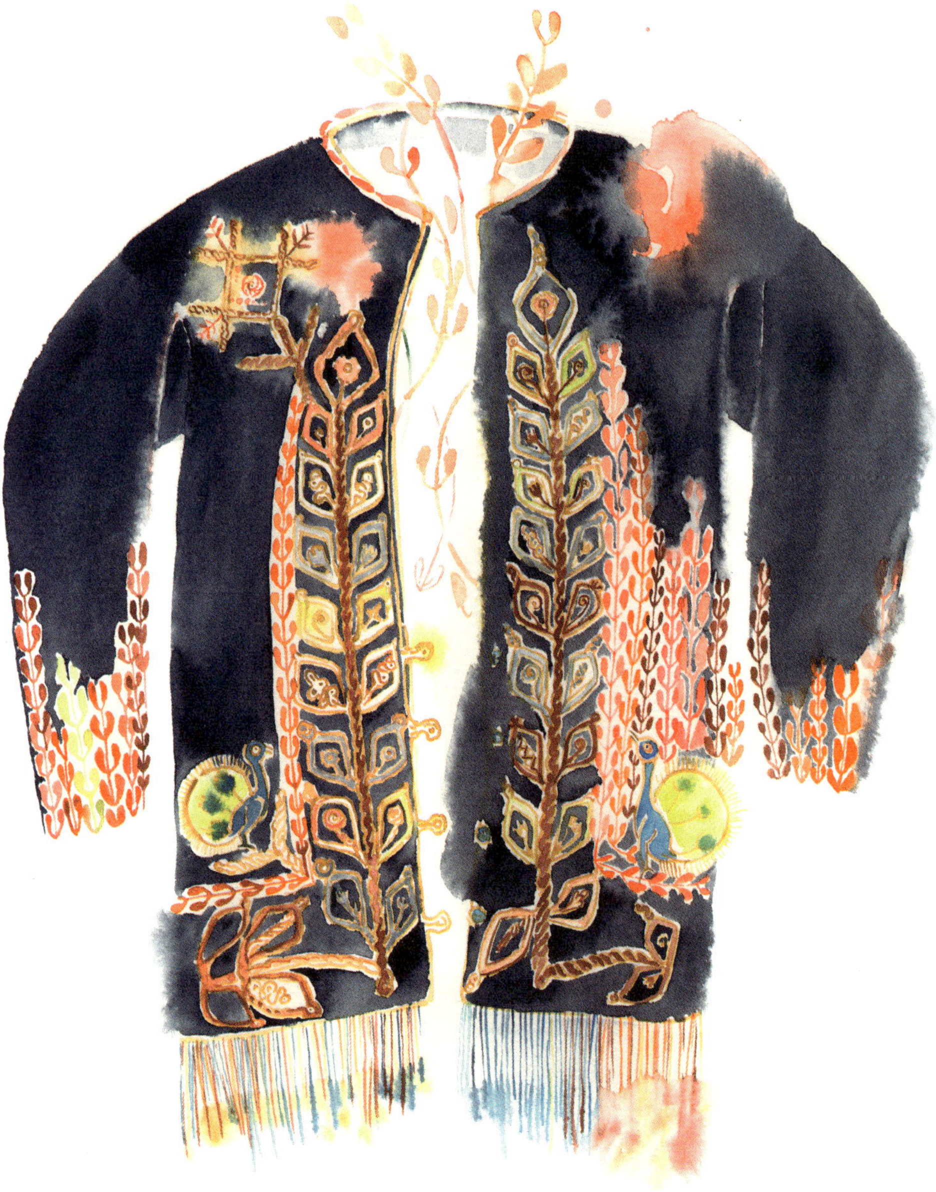

Joseph Interprets Dreams

Joseph's brothers sold him to traders, and they took him to Egypt, where one of Pharaoh's most trusted men bought him and sent him to serve in Pharaoh's palace. Because Joseph was very wise and good, he became the servant in charge of Pharaoh's household. He was living a very good life in Egypt.

Joseph was a good-looking man, and eventually the Pharaoh's wife became interested in him. He refused to have an affair with her, of course, because he was a godly man. She grew very angry, and pretended that he had attacked her; Pharaoh believed his wife, and threw Joseph into prison.

God loved Joseph, so no matter where Joseph went, God showed the people that he was a good man, and they treated him well. The prison master soon put him in charge of the whole prison and its prisoners.

God gave Joseph a special gift so that he could understand dreams; in the prison, people sometimes had interesting dreams, and Joseph could always explain what they meant.

One day Pharaoh had a dream he could not understand: he was standing by a river, and suddenly seven fat cows came up out of the river, and then after them, seven skinny cows came out of the river. The skinny cows ate the fat cows!

Then Pharaoh had another dream much like the first: seven plump ears of corn appeared, and then seven skinny ears of corn appeared – and the skinny corn ate up all the fat corn!

Pharaoh thought these were very strange dreams, so he called for all the wise men of Egypt. He told them his dreams, but no one could guess what they meant. Then one of his servants mentioned that in the prison, his old servant Joseph was doing such a good job explaining everyone's dreams. Right away, they called for Joseph to come out of the dungeon to interpret Pharoah's strange dreams.

So Joseph came back to the palace, and he explained that God had shown him the meaning of the dreams: Egypt would have seven very good years with plentiful harvests, but then after that, there would be seven bad years, where the harvest would dry up. The people might starve during these terrible years. So Joseph explained that God was telling Pharaoh to save the harvest from the good years, so that Egypt would have food during the bad years.

Pharaoh saw that the spirit of God was in Joseph, so he put Joseph in charge of all of Egypt. Joseph made sure that everyone stored up the food during the first seven years, so that they would not starve during the bad years.

Questions:

How did Joseph know what people's dreams meant? God told Joseph the meaning of dreams.

What did Pharaoh's dreams mean? Pharaoh's dreams were about how seven good years (fat cows or ears of corn) would be swallowed up by seven very bad years (skinny cows or ears of corn). It meant that Egypt would need to store up food during the good years, so that they would have something to eat during the bad years.

Why did Pharaoh trust Joseph to be in charge of Egypt? Pharaoh believed that Joseph was wise, and saw that God was blessing him. He wanted God to bless Egypt too, so he put Joseph in charge.

Advanced Discussion Idea:

God takes care of Joseph wherever he goes: first, he blesses him with his father's love, and then when Joseph is sold into slavery, God gives him a good position in Pharaoh's house. Even when Pharaoh's wife lies and has him thrown into prison, he is blessed with the gift of interpreting dreams and finds his way back to being in charge of Egypt. God never abandons Joseph, even though sometimes it seems that very bad things are happening to him.

Scripture references:
Genesis, chapters 39 through 41

Joseph and His Family

Joseph lead Egypt for seven years of abundant harvests; he showed everyone how to store up grain and other foods. Then the bad years came: the harvests dried up and people everywhere were starving, except in Egypt, where they still had food saved up.

The famine also reached the land of Canaan, where Joseph's brothers and his father Jacob lived. The family ran out of food and needed help. Jacob heard that there was food in Egypt, so he sent ten of his sons – all except for the young Benjamin – to go to Egypt to buy some grain. Of course they didn't know that their long-lost Joseph was now in charge of Egypt, and would be the man in charge of selling the grain.

Joseph did not tell them who he was at first, but when they came he asked them many questions. He knew who they were, but he pretended to think that they were spies. He said that they must prove they were not spies, by leaving one of them to stay in his prison house while the others went home to get their youngest brother, Benjamin, whom Joseph loved very much. They bought their grain, and left one brother behind.

When the brothers were heading home, they realized that the Egyptians had given them grain, but had also put their money back in the sacks! They were very worried that the Egyptians would think they had stolen from them.

They returned home, and told their father what happened. He did not want to send Benjamin with them; he had already lost Joseph and was worried that he might lose Benjamin too. But when after a year the food had run out, there was no choice.

The brothers brought Benjamin to Egypt – and they also brought gifts of honey and myrrh for the man who sold them the food, and they brought all of the money from the first year plus more money for the new grain they would buy.

When Joseph saw that they brought his brother Benjamin to him, he asked his servants to prepare a large meal for everyone at Joseph's home. The brothers were worried that the Egyptians would be angry that they had not left any money the first year, and they explained to Joseph's servants and tried to pay the money again. The servants were very forgiving and kind, and they brought out the brother they had left behind.

Joseph came home, and asked about how their father was doing, whether he was still alive, and he was happy to hear that Jacob was well. As they spoke to him, his brothers bowed down – just as they had in Joseph's dreams long ago. They all shared a wonderful meal together, but as the brothers left, Joseph asked his servants to hide a silver cup in Benjamin's bag. Later, they chased the brothers down and pretended that Benjamin had stolen the cup!

Joseph told the brothers that Benjamin would have to stay in Egypt as his servant, but the brothers explained that their father had already lost his beloved son, and could not bear to lose Benjamin too! Finally, Joseph's heart was breaking and he had to tell them the truth.

He said, "I am Joseph your brother, whom you sold into Egypt. Now do not be angry with yourselves because you sold me; for God sent me here to save lives. This is the second year of famine and there will be five more years. It was not you who sent me here, but God; and He made me ruler throughout all the land of Egypt. Hurry then and go to my father and tell him everything, and bring him to me."

Joseph arranged a place for his father and brothers to live nearby and he made sure that they had food during the terrible famine. So in the end, it was good that Joseph was in Egypt, because God helped him save his family and many other people from death.

Questions:

Why did Joseph's brothers come to Egypt? Why didn't they bring Benjamin? Joseph's brothers came to buy grain, because they were had no food back home. Jacob kept Benjamin at home, so that nothing would happen to him.

How did Joseph make the brothers look like thieves two times?
First he had their money put back into the sacks, as if they had taken the grain for free, then he made it look like Benjamin had stolen his silver cup.

Did Joseph forgive his brothers for selling him to the traders?
Yes, Joseph forgave them and said that God had caused it to happen, so that Joseph could make sure that his family and so many others did not starve during the seven bad years.

Advanced Discussion Idea:

Joseph was betrayed by his brothers and sent as a slave into prison, and yet his time there allowed him to save his family and so many other people from a terrible death. The Fathers say that this is like Jesus Christ, who was betrayed and went into the prison of Hades, so that He could trample down death by death. Like Jesus, Joseph did not complain and forgave those who harmed him.

Scripture References:
Genesis chapters 42 through 46

Jacob's Prophecy

When Jacob was very old and was dying, he called his sons to give them blessings, just as his father Isaac had once given blessings before he died. Jacob said, "Gather together, so that I may tell you what will happen to each of you."

When it was Judah's turn, Jacob said:

"Judah, your brothers will praise you;
Your hand shall be on the neck of your enemies;
Your father's sons will bow down before you.
Judah is a lion's cub;
My son, you have grown up.
You bow down, and you sleep as a lion and a cub;
And who shall wake him?
The scepter shall stay with Judah,
And to Him shall be the expectation of the nations.
Binding his colt to a vine,
And his donkey's colt to its branch,
He will wash his garments in wine,
And his clothes in the blood of grapes."

Jacob's blessing for Judah talks about how Judah is like a cub that has grown up into a lion. The lion is the 'king of the jungle' so when we say that someone is like a lion, we are saying they are like a king. He also says that 'the scepter shall stay with Judah', and a scepter is something that king would hold: it's like a golden stick with jewels on top, and rulers hold it to show that they are in charge. Judah and his tribe will always be in charge, so the scepter will always be with them.

Jesus, the King of Kings, would be born through the line of Judah. So Jacob is talking about lots of kings and rulers, but he is especially talking about Jesus. When he is talking about a donkey or a donkey's colt, he is prophesying or foretelling us that Jesus will ride on a donkey's colt as He enters triumphantly into Jerusalem on Palm Sunday.

It's also important to know that God gave Jacob a new name: He called him, "Israel". His twelve sons each had so many children that they each became a tribe, and they were called the twelve tribes of Israel. Judah's tribe always had the scepter – it was the ruling tribe of Israel.

Questions:

Which of Jacob's sons would be the one who carried on Abraham's great legacy? Though Joseph ruled in Egypt, it was Judah who led the family and would become the father of nations, and eventually the King of Kings would come from his line.

What does it mean when Jacob says that the scepter shall stay with Judah? A scepter is something that a ruler holds, like a stick with beautiful decorations. Judah would rule over his brothers. In fact, each of the twelve brothers would become a whole tribe of people, often called the twelve tribes of Israel, and the tribe of Judah would rule over the others.

Jacob is telling us that Judah's tribe will be full of rulers and kings. Who is the most important King who will come from this line? The King of Kings, Jesus Christ.

Advanced Discussion Idea:

Jacob's blessing for Judah is a prophecy: this means that Jacob is telling us important things about the future. He is announcing that the Son of God will become man through the tribe of Judah. Judah has the 'expectation of the nations' because the whole world is waiting for its salvation, which will come through the line of Judah in the form of Jesus Christ. The lion who sleeps ('and who shall wake him?') is Jesus on Holy Saturday – the king who dies and goes to Hades. No one will wake him, because He is God and He will wake Himself up from death. The references to wine remind us of the blood of Jesus in Holy Communion, and the donkey colt is a prophecy about how the Son of God will ride into Jerusalem on Palm Sunday.

Scripture references: *Genesis 49: 1-2, 8-12*

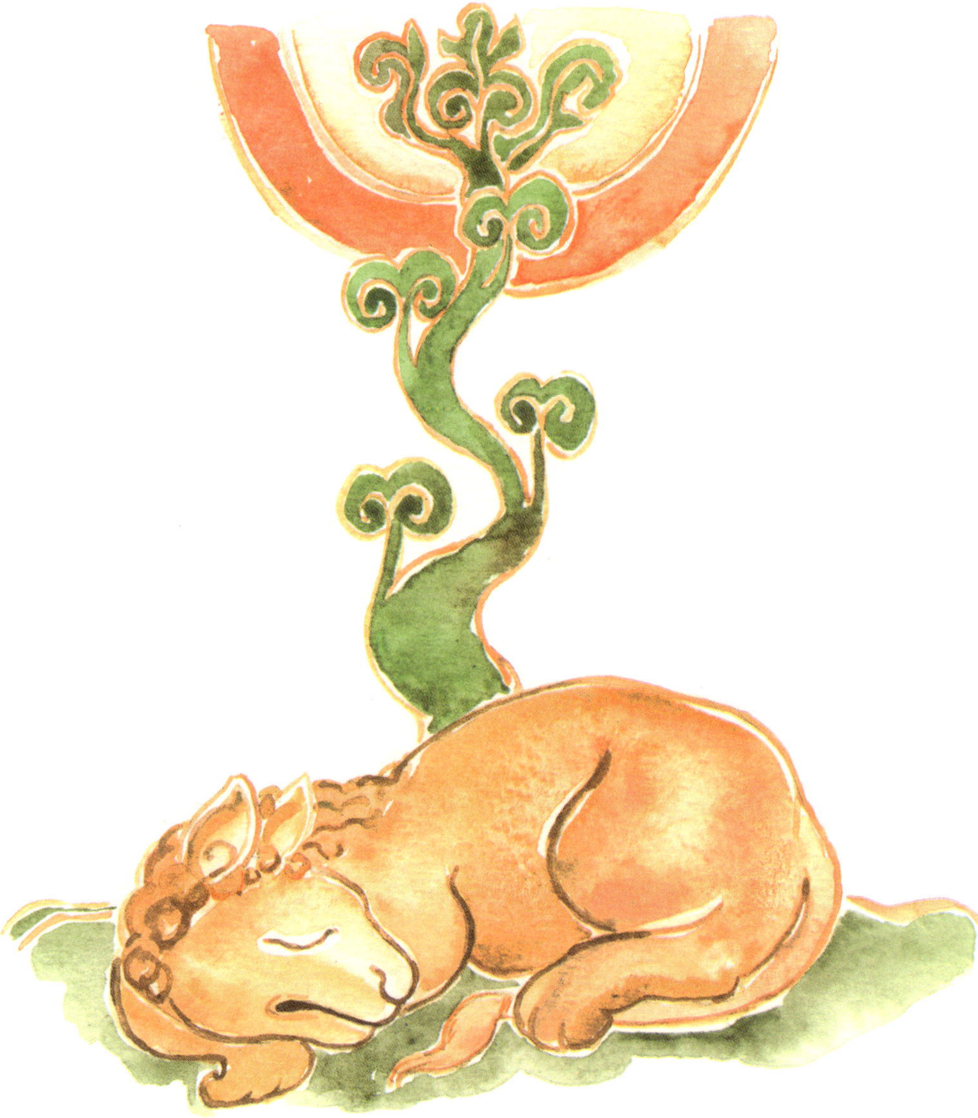

The Prophet Moses

The Pharaoh of Egypt loved Joseph so he gave him a place of honor. But many years later, a new Pharaoh rose in Egypt, and he didn't remember Joseph and his family. To him, the people of Israel were just workers, and he needed them to stay and work – but he worried that if there were too many of them, they might join up with Egypt's enemies and fight against them, and maybe even leave Egypt completely. Pharaoh came up with a plan to make the Israelites stop growing: he commanded all his people, saying, "Every boy born to the Israelites you shall cast into the river, but every female you shall save alive."

One of the men of Israel and his wife had a new baby son, and they hid him for three months. They didn't want anyone to hurt him. But when she could no longer hide him, the mother made a little ark out of bulrushes, dabbed it with asphalt to make it waterproof, and put the child in it, laying it in the reeds by the river's bank.

Then the daughter of Pharaoh came down to bathe at the river, and she saw the ark among the reeds, and sent a maid to get it. When she opened the ark, she saw the child crying, and the daughter of Pharaoh had compassion on him and said, "This is one of the Israelite children."

Then the child's sister said to Pharaoh's daughter, "Shall I go and call a nurse for you from the Israelite women, that she may nurse the child for you?" Pharaoh's daughter agreed, and the maiden went and called the child's mother. Pharaoh's daughter then said to her, "Take this child and nurse him for me, and I will pay you." So the baby's own mother took him and nursed him, as if she were his nanny.

When the boy grew up, she brought him to Pharaoh's daughter, and he became her son; and she called his name Moses, which meant that he had been taken out of the water.

One day, Moses saw a bush that was burning with fire, but the bush was not turning into black ashes – it was not consumed, but instead it was still green and healthy.

Moses found this very interesting, and he turned to get a better look. When the Lord saw that he was interested and looking, God called to him from inside the bush and said, "Moses! Moses!" Then Moses answered, "Here I am."

God said, "Do not come any closer. Take your sandals off your feet, for the place where you stand is holy ground. I am the God of your father—the God of Abraham, the God of Isaac, and the God of Jacob."

Moses hid his face, for he was afraid to look at God.

Then the Lord said, "I have seen the suffering of My people in Egypt, and have heard their cry. I came down to lead them out of Egypt; I will send you to Pharaoh, to bring My people, the children of Israel, out of Egypt."

Moses was very humble, and did not know why he would be chosen as the leader, but God promised that He would help him.

So Moses said, "When I go to the children of Israel and say to them, 'The God of your fathers sent me to you,' and they ask me, 'What is His name?' what shall I tell them?"

God said, "I AM; I am the Existing One. Thus you shall say to the children of Israel: 'The Existing One sent me to you. The Lord God of your fathers—the God of Abraham, the God of Isaac, and the God of Jacob—sent me to you.' They will listen to you and you shall go with the elders of Israel, to the king of Egypt; and you shall say to him, 'Our God met with us; and now, let us go three days' journey into the desert to sacrifice to our God.' But I know Pharaoh will not let you go. Thus I will stretch out My hand and strike the Egyptians with all My wonders which I will work among them; and after that he will let you go."

Questions:

What was life like for the tribes of Israel in Egypt? It was hard – the Egyptians were making them work very hard, and being cruel.

God promised that Abraham's seed would be so many that they could not be counted, like the stars. The tribes of Israel were growing in number. What rule did Pharaoh make to keep them from growing so quickly? He ordered that all of the male children should be killed, so that there would be no more Hebrew boys.

Moses' mother put him into an ark on the river, so that no one would kill her son. Who did the Pharaoh's daughter hire to be his nanny, taking care of him until he was grown? Moses' own mother was able to take care of him, pretending to be his nurse, until he was grown and went to live as the son of Pharaoh's daughter.

What was so interesting about the bush that Moses saw? The bush was on fire and burning, but instead of turning the bush all black and ashy, the fire was burning without consuming it; the bush stayed green and healthy.

Who spoke to Moses from the bush and what did He want Moses to say to Pharaoh? He was God, 'the existing One' and he

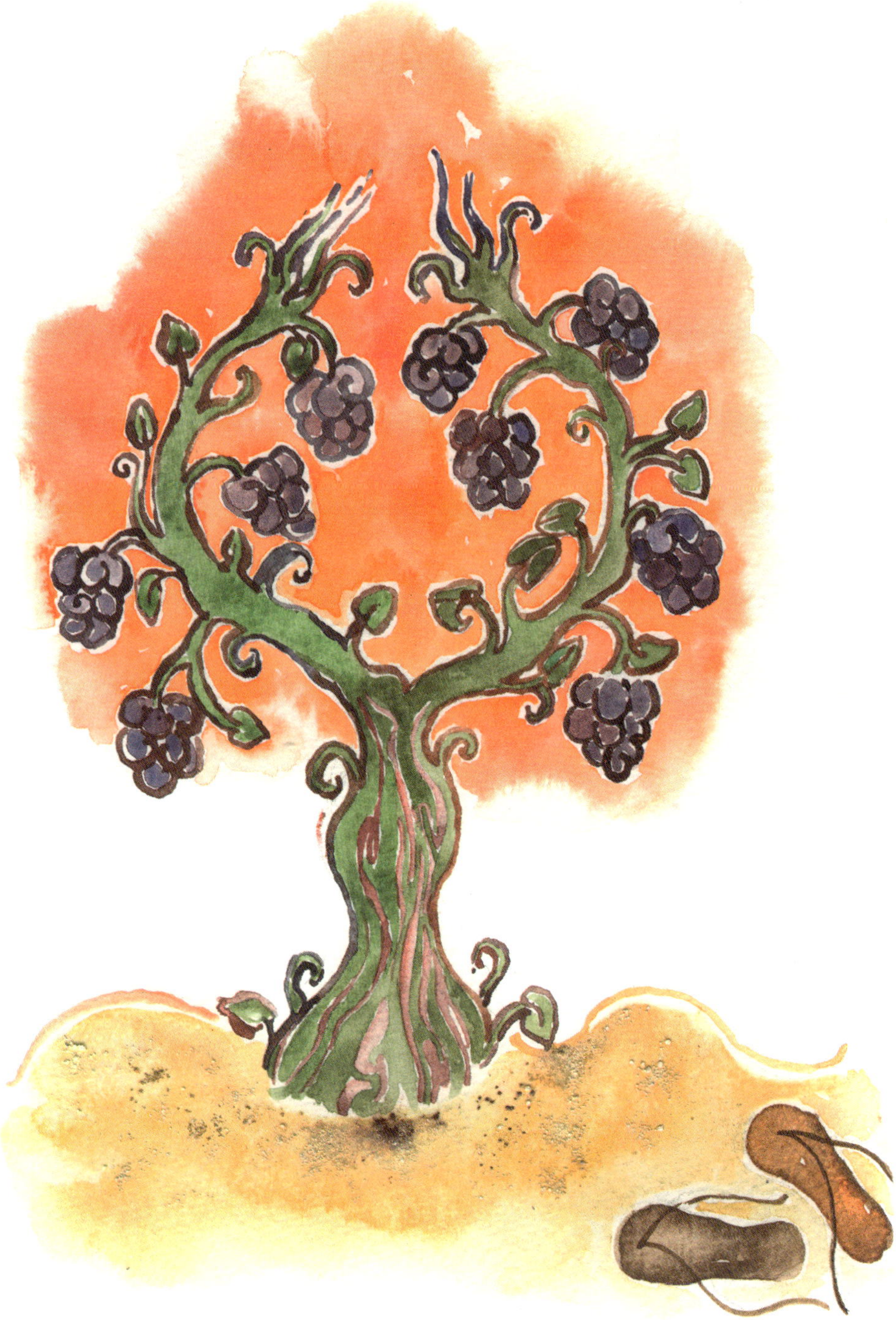

requested that Moses tell Pharaoh that their God met with them and wants them to go three days' walk into the desert to sacrifice to Him.

Advanced Discussion Idea:

You may have noticed that the word for the basket baby Moses was placed in is 'ark', just like the ark that Noah built. An ark is something that carries things safely – God made sure that an ark carried His good people safely through the Flood, and that an ark carried his Prophet Moses on the water. Later, we will see more arks, including the Ark of the Covenant and even the Holy Theotokos (who was the ark that carried Jesus safely).

The Holy Church is the ark that carries us safely through the difficulties of this world. In fact the church building is divided into three parts: the altar (where Father prepares holy communion), the narthex (where we enter the church and light candles, preparing ourselves to worship) and the nave (the main room where the people stand during services). The word 'nave' comes from 'navem or navis' which means boat. We think of the church building as a boat or an ark that carries us safely through our journey.

In our pre-communion prayers, we see that Holy Communion is a 'fire that burns the unworthy'. God can burn through us like He burns through the bush: He is the fire that will burn away the parts that are not good (like sins) but He will leave us stronger and more alive than ever.

The burning bush also offers a promise for the future: Mary, the Holy Mother of God, is like that bush, for she has God within her, and even though she is filled with His fiery presence, she is never consumed or damaged in any way.

Scripture references:
Exodus 1: 8-22, 2: 1-10, 3: 1-20

Leaving Egypt

The Lord told Moses, "Go, tell Pharaoh to send the children of Israel out from his land." But Moses didn't think that Pharaoh would listen to him, because he had a terrible stutter and he was not good at making speeches, so God allowed him to bring his brother Aaron along to help him.

Moses and Aaron asked Pharaoh to let the Israelites leave Egypt, but he refused. So God announced that He would send many plagues down on Egypt. Each time, Moses and Aaron would warn Pharaoh that he must let the Israelites leave or a terrible plague would come, but each time Pharaoh would refuse. God would then send down something very bad, like turning all of the water in Egypt to blood, or covering the land with frogs or with flies or locusts – and every time, Pharaoh would say that the Israelites could leave, and then as soon as the plague stopped his heart was hardened again and he would not let them go.

God sent a final, terrible plague: He would kill the firstborn son of every Egyptian family. He instructed the Israelites to sacrifice firstborn lambs, and to paint their doors with the blood of the lambs, so that death would pass over them. This was called the 'passover' or the 'Pascha'.

Again Moses and Aaron warned Pharaoh that he must let the Israelites go, or this terrible tragedy would happen – but Pharaoh's heart was hardened and he would not let them go.

The Israelites painted the blood on their doors and waited. At midnight there was great cry in all the land of Egypt, for all of the firstborn sons had suddenly died – but the firstborn sons of the Israelites were safe. Pharaoh ordered them to leave immediately, to take everything they owned and to leave Egypt.

The Israelites hurried away – a huge procession of all the children of Israel, fleeing from Egypt together. God lead them Himself: He was a pillar of clouds by day, and a pillar of fire by night, so that they could follow Him out of Egypt, to the promised land. He lead them to the edge of the Red Sea, where they set up camp.

Once again, as he had so many times before, Pharaoh thought again about whether he wanted to allow his workers to leave Egypt; once again, his heart was hardened and he decided to keep them. He loaded up his armies into chariots, and they raced into the desert to capture the Israelites and bring them back to Egypt.

When the Israelites saw that the armies of Egypt were coming for them, they were frightened. But the pillar of cloud moved between them and the Egyptians, and Moses stretched out his hand over the sea and the Lord sent a strong south wind all that night and made the sea dry ground. The sea was divided, with a dry path right through the center of it.

So the children of Israel walked right through the middle of the sea on the dry ground, and the waters were like walls to them on their right and on their left.

Then the Egyptian armies – all of Pharaoh's horses and chariots – followed them into the middle of the sea, but God slowed them down. He made the axles of their chariots stop turning, so that they struggled to move forward there in the Red Sea.

Then, once the Israelites were safe on the shore, the Lord said to Moses, "Stretch out your hand over the sea so the waters may come back upon the Egyptians."

So Moses stretched out his hand over the sea; and the waters returned and covered the chariots, the horsemen, and all of Pharaoh's army. Not a single one remained. The Lord saved Israel from the Egyptians, and the people of Israel believed in God and trusted His servant Moses.

Questions:

Why didn't Moses want to be God's spokesman? Moses had a very difficult stutter, so he was not comfortable making big speeches.

Moses and Aaron kept warning Pharaoh that plagues were coming. What did Pharaoh have to do to save Egypt from the plagues? He had to let the people of Israel go free.

How did the Israelites mark their houses so that the plague of death would pass over them? They would sacrifice a firstborn lamb, and paint its blood on the doorway.

Advanced Discussion Idea:

Moses begged God to find a better spokesman, a more worthy prophet. He had a speech impediment and thought that no one would listen to him. But God wasn't looking for a slick salesman with a silver tongue: He was happy to be represented by an imperfect, stuttering man. When God works through us, it is God's strength and His grace that shine through, not ours.

Scripture references: *Exodus chapters 6 through 14*

ST
PRO
PHET

MOSES

57

In the Wilderness

*M*oses lead the people of Israel from the Red Sea into the wilderness. For three days they traveled through the desert and found no water to drink. Finally, they came to a place where there was water, but it was bitter; it tasted terrible, and they could not drink it. Then the people complained about Moses, frustrated that he had lead them to such a bad place. They cried out, "What shall we drink?"

Moses cried to the Lord, and the Lord showed him a tree. When he cast it into the waters, the waters became sweet. Moses explained to the people, "If you listen to the Lord your God and follow His commandments, He will take care of you. The Lord your God heals you."

They continued on their journey, into the wilderness. It had been about 45 days since they left Egypt, and all of the children of Israel were complaining about Moses and Aaron. They would say, "Back in Egypt, we had plenty of meat and bread, but you brought us out into this desert to starve all of us to death."

The Lord heard their complaints and He took care of them. He told Moses that He would rain down food for them: 'manna' or bread in the mornings, and meat in the evenings. He said that the people should go out and gather as much as they needed every day, but not more. They shouldn't try to store it overnight, but instead they should trust that He would send more the next day. There was one exception: on the sixth day of every week, they could gather double so that on the Sabbath they could rest.

Moses told them not to try to save any overnight, but many of them did not listen. Some of them tried to save some manna until morning, and it bred worms and it stank. So Moses was frustrated with them.

On the sixth day, they gathered twice as much bread, because the next day was the Sabbath, and you couldn't do any work on the Sabbath; it was the day of rest. So for that day, they did save the manna for the next morning and this time it did not stink or get wormy.

Some of the people went out on the Sabbath day to gather manna, but there wasn't any. God only sent it on the other days of the week; on the day of rest, nothing came down, so that they would rest.

As they traveled, they came again to a place without water, and the people complained against Moses again, saying, "Why did you bring us up out of Egypt to kill us, our children, and our cattle with thirst?"

So Moses cried out to the Lord, saying, "What shall I do with these people?"

Then the Lord said to Moses, "Go before this people and strike the rock with your staff, and water will come out of it so the people may drink." So Moses did that, and God provided water for them again.

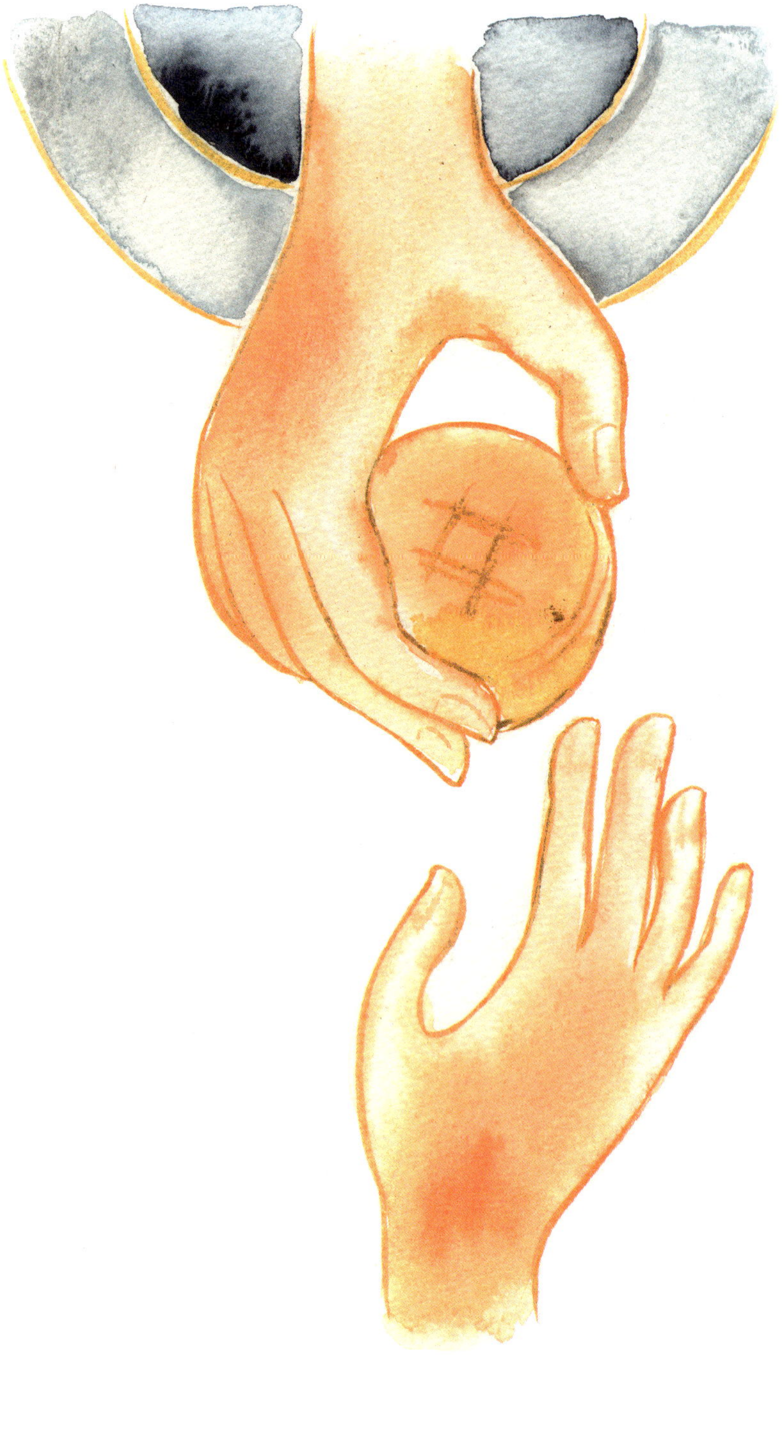

Questions:

As the children of Israel followed Moses through the wilderness, how did God take care of them? He sent 'manna' (bread) and meat for them, and He provided good water to drink when they had none.

What would happen if they tried to keep the food until the next day? On most days, it would rot and be filled with worms if it was kept overnight, but on the Sabbath it would always stay good for the next day. God wanted them to rest on the Sabbath.

Why is the seventh day the Sabbath? Because when He was making the earth, God rested on the seventh day. He teaches us that it's good to rest.

When the people couldn't find water, what would they say to Moses? What would God do? The Israelites would complain very often, saying that Moses brought them out into the desert to die of thirst. God would always provide them water to drink, even out from stones in a desert!

Advanced Discussion Idea:

In the wilderness, the Israelites were tired and frustrated. They kept accusing Moses of leading them to misery, even though they saw God lead them as a pillar of cloud and a pillar of fire. God parted the Red Sea and swallowed up the Egyptian armies to protect them, but just a few weeks later they acted like that was no big deal. God would miraculously take care of His people, but they complained anyway. The Israelites' journey helps us to understand our own journey: we struggle on our path, and even though God sends us blessings and miracles, we complain and forget to be grateful.

Later, Jesus explained that He is the bread of life, the true manna sent from heaven (John 6:30-35) and that He is the living water (John 4:6-15). Just as God once sent bread and water to the Israelites in the desert, He sends Jesus to all of us now. Those who believe in Jesus Christ shall never hunger or thirst again, because they will live on the bread of life and the living water.

Scripture references: *Exodus 15:22-17:1-7*

God's Law

The people of Israel journeyed to the Sinai Desert, and Moses went up to the mountain of God. On the mountain, God said, "Tell the children of Israel: 'You have seen what I did to the Egyptians, and how I have taken care of you. If you will obey My voice and keep My law, you shall be a special people to Me; you shall be a royal priesthood and a holy nation.'" So Moses told them what God said and they all agreed: "Everything the Lord said we will do." So they agreed to be God's special nation.

God told Moses to tell the people to get ready. On the third day, He would visit them: He would appear again as a pillar of cloud, descending on Mt. Sinai. So the people got ready.

On the third day in the morning, there were thunderings and lightnings and a dark cloud on Mount Sinai; and the sound of the trumpet was very loud, and all the people in the camp trembled. Mount Sinai was completely covered in smoke, because God descended upon it in fire. Its smoke went up like the smoke of a furnace, and the people were amazed. And when the blast of the trumpet sounded long and became louder and louder, Moses spoke, and God answered him by voice. Then the Lord came down upon Mount Sinai, on the top of the mountain, and He called Moses to the top of the mountain, and Moses went up.

Now the Lord gave Moses ten commandments for the people of God to follow:
- You shall have no other gods before Me.
- You shall not make false idols and worship them.
- You shall not take the name of the Lord your God in vain.
- Remember the Sabbath Day, and keep it holy.
- Honor your father and mother.
- You shall not murder.
- You shall not commit adultery.
- You shall not steal.
- You shall not bear false witness against your neighbor.
- You shall not covet your neighbor's wife or his house, or whatever belongs to your neighbor.

Then Moses went back up the mountain and stayed for forty days and forty nights with the Lord, and the Lord instructed him on many things, including how to build the Ark of the Covenant. This was a wooden box covered in gold and decorated with beautiful golden cherubim. Like Noah's ark, God told Moses exactly how to build it: what materials to use, exactly what size it should be, and how it should be designed and decorated. Inside this box, they would keep some of the manna God had sent down to them and also the ten commandments, and everything that God told them to put there. God would speak to them through the ark.

Questions:

God invited the people of Israel to be His special nation among all the earth. What would they have to do if they were His special nation? They have to obey Him and keep His law – like following the ten commandments and other rules He would make for them.

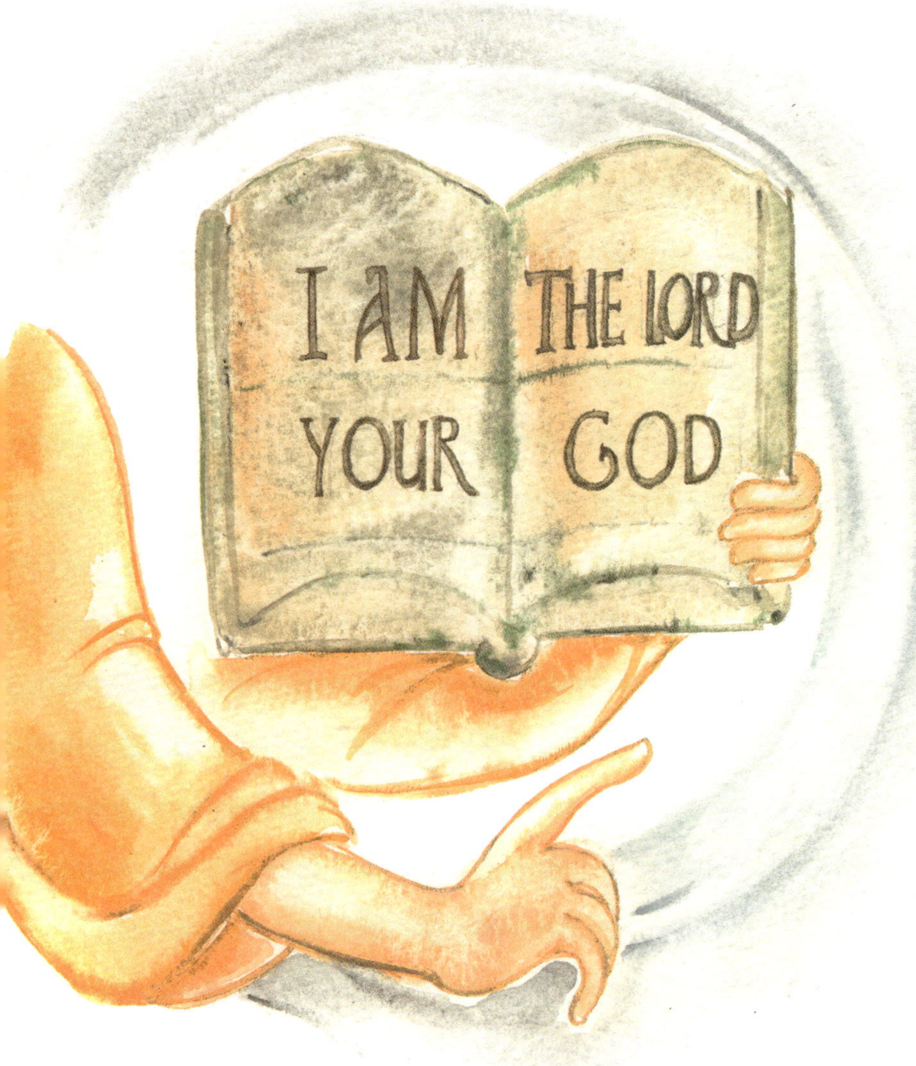
I AM THE LORD
YOUR GOD

How did God appear to them? He descended like a cloud on the mountain, with thunder and loud trumpets. He was fire, so the smoke covered the whole mountain, and the smoke rose up into the sky. (This must be like the pillar of cloud and fire they followed out of Egypt.)

Would God stay with them and speak to them again? Yes. He gave them specific instructions for building the Ark of the Covenant, and He would speak to them through the Ark in the future. He promised to stay with them and take care of them.

Advanced Discussion Idea:

An ark is something that carries something special, protecting it. God told Noah exactly how to build the ark that would protect his family and all of the animals during the Great Flood, and then He told Moses exactly how to build the ark that would keep God close to the people of Israel. The Ark of the Covenant does not carry people, but it carries God and the blessings He has given His people.

The Holy Theotokos is sometimes compared to the Ark of the Covenant, because she carries Jesus in her womb, bringing Him to His people.

Scripture references:
Exodus, chapters 19 and 20, 25 and 26

Joshua and the Battle of Jericho

When Moses was very old, he died, but the Israelites were still wandering in the wilderness, so God chose Joshua to lead His people to the land He had promised them, which was waiting for them on the other side of the Jordan River.

There were already people living on the land, so Joshua and the Israelites would have to conquer the city of Jericho to make it their own. First, Joshua sent two young men to spy on the city, so that they could tell him what it was like there. The spies looked around Jericho and then went into the house of a harlot named Rahab and spent the night there. Rahab knew that they were spies, but she also knew how their God had led them out of Egypt and parted the Red Sea, so she respected the One True God and she wanted to be an ally of His people.

The king of Jericho heard that there were spies in town, and that they had gone into Rahab's house. So he sent his men, and they knocked on the door and told Rahab to hand over the spies. But Rahab protected them, saying, "These men came to me; but as the city gate was being shut last night, they left. I don't know where they went. Perhaps if you hurry you can catch them." But really, she had them hidden on her roof.

Before the spies went to sleep that night, Rahab went up on the roof and said, "I know that the Lord will give you this city, for we heard how He parted the Red Sea for you when you came out of Egypt, and we were amazed in our heart, for your God is in heaven above and on earth below. Now swear to me by the Lord God that just as I was merciful to you, you will also be merciful to me and you will protect my family."

The spies agreed, "We promise you, and we ask you to set a sign; hang this scarlet cord in the window, then gather yourself and your family into your house. We will protect whoever is with you in your house." The spies left, and the king's men never found them; the spies went back to Joshua and told him everything they had learned.

God told Joshua to take His people to the Jordan River. Twelve priests walked into the river first, carrying the ark of the covenant. When their feet touched the water of the Jordan River, suddenly the river stopped flowing! The land under their feet dried up, and all the children of Israel crossed on dry ground.

The city of Jericho had a wall all around it, to protect it. Armies could not attack Jericho, because they could not get through that wall. So the Lord said to Joshua, "Behold, I will deliver Jericho into your hand. Position your soldiers around the city wall, and when you sound the trumpet, let all the people shout together, and when they shout, the walls of the city shall fall down and your people will run in."

Every day the Israelite priests and the soldiers and all of the people marched around the city. When Joshua told them to shout, they all shouted together. For six days they did this.

On the seventh day, they rose early in the morning and walked around the city six times. Then as they marched around the seventh time, the priests blew the trumpets, and Joshua said to the people, "Shout, for indeed the Lord has handed over the city to you. This city is cursed by the Lord, except for Rahab the harlot and everyone who is in her house."

So the priests sounded the trumpets, and all the people shouted together with one great and mighty shout. Then the entire wall fell down, and all the Israelite people ran into the city.

Then Joshua said to the two spies, "Go into the house of the woman, and bring her out with her family." So they brought out Rahab and all her family, and they allowed her to dwell in Israel to this very day, because she protected the spies Joshua sent to Jericho.

Questions:

Why did Rahab protect the spies who came into her house? Rahab had heard about how the Lord parted the Red Sea and took such good care of His people, and she realized that He was mighty. She wanted to be a friend of God's people, so that He would take care of her too.

When the Israelites were ready to cross the Jordan River, the priests went first with the ark of the covenant. What happened when their feet were in the river? The river stopped flowing, and the ground dried up so that all of Israel could easily cross.

The Israelites marched around Jericho and let up a great shout. Why did the wall fall down? God showed everyone that He wanted the Israelites to have the city of Jericho by doing this miracle for them; the noise of their shout did not tear down the walls, but God tore down the walls for them. Joshua and the Israelites trusted God and did what He said to do, and He fulfilled His promise by making the walls fall down.

Advanced Discussion Idea:

Rahab was not one of God's Israelites, but she learned about God and chose to serve Him and His people. She was amazed in her heart to hear how God had parted the Red Sea for His people; she understood that He was truly God over both heaven and earth. She betrayed her own people and their gods by protecting the spies; she abandoned her own people in order to serve God and His people. Rahab was rewarded by being allowed to live in Israel, but she also received another reward: she was given a place in the line of Christ. A man named Salmon from the line of Judah had a son with Rahab, namcd Boaz. Rahab's son was the next in the family line – that same line promised to Abraham and Isaac, to Jacob and Judah. Rahab, a harlot from Jericho, became a part of that royal line that lead to the king of kings, for God loves all people, and includes all of us in His family.

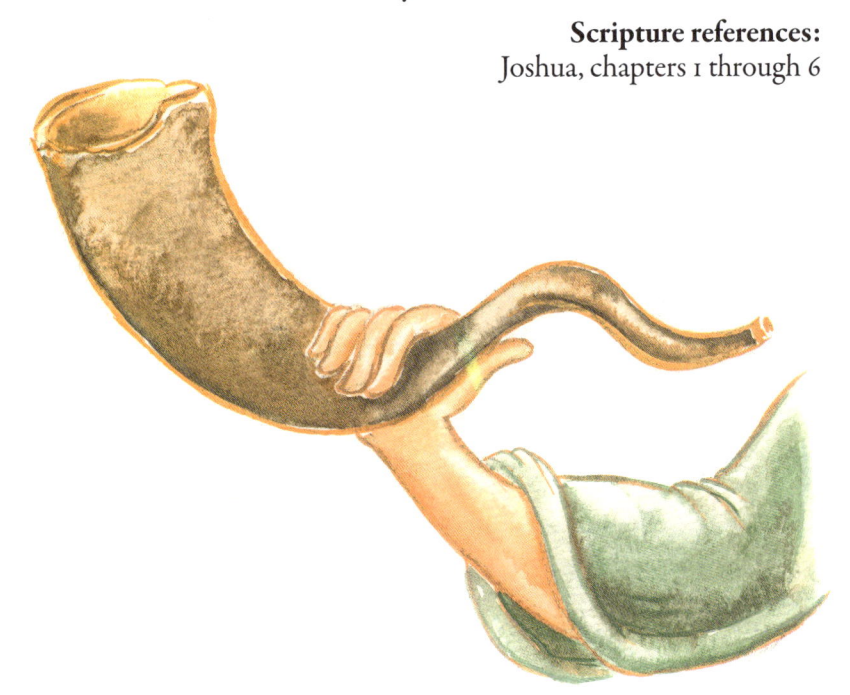

Scripture references:
Joshua, chapters 1 through 6

Ruth's Story

There was a woman from Bethlehem named Naomi. She and her husband lived far from home in Moab with their two grown sons. Naomi's husband died, and both of her sons married Moabite women – so they were not from the tribes of Israel, but came from families that worshipped other gods. One of the women was named Orpah, and the other was Ruth.

For about ten years, Naomi lived with her sons and their wives, but then both of her sons died. She was a widow and now Orpah and Ruth were widows too. Naomi decided to leave Moab and go back to her family in Bethlehem, and she told her two daughters-in-law to go back to their families too.

They cried, sorry to see her move away, and they said, "We will return with you to your people." But Naomi said, "No, no. You should go back to your homes and to your old gods. I have no more sons to marry you, and nothing to offer you."

Orpah kissed her mother-in-law goodbye and returned to her people and her gods. But Ruth said, "Do not ask me to leave you, or turn back from following you; for wherever you go, I will go; your people shall be my people, and your God, my God."

Naomi and Ruth went to Bethlehem, but they had no way to make a living. So Ruth asked Naomi if she could go into the fields after they were already harvested and find whatever grains might be left over. Naomi agreed, and she went to work in the fields.

    She happened to come to some fields that were owned by Boaz, who also came from Naomi's family. In fact, Boaz was the grandson of the harlot Rahab, who had protected the spies when they came into Jericho. Boaz asked his servants who this young woman was, and they explained that Ruth was a young Moabite woman who came back with Naomi. She worked very hard from sunrise to sunset, never stopping to rest. Boaz was impressed because she was such a hard worker, but also because she was not an Israelite but she chose to follow God and to be part of His people, and because she was taking care of Naomi as if she were her own mother.

    Boaz told Ruth that she could stay close and work in his fields, and that his workers would make sure she was protected and safe. She was very grateful for his kindness.

Soon, Boaz and Ruth were married, and she gave birth to a son, who she named Obed. Obed would have a son named Jesse, and Jesse's son would David, the king. From David's line would come Jesus Himself! So Ruth found her place in the family line that would bring the King of Kings, even though she was not even born in the tribes of Israel. She came from another nation, but she loved God and followed Him, and she loved Naomi and took care of her, so God rewarded her with a wonderful place in the line of the people of Abraham, Isaac, and Jacob.

Questions:

Why did Naomi tell Orpah and Ruth to go home to their mothers? Because all three of them were widows, and Naomi had nothing to give her daughters-in-law. She could not take care of them.

Why did Ruth stay with Naomi? Ruth declared that she would take care of Naomi forever, and that she would follow Naomi's God and be a part of Naomi's people. She basically converted to become part of the tribes of Israel, and refused to leave them.

Why did Boaz like Ruth? Ruth was a hard worker, and she was very loyal and good to Naomi. Boaz liked that she had decided to follow God and to become a part of the Israelite people even though she wasn't born into the nation of Israel.

Advanced Discussion Idea:
Ruth was not born into the tribes of Israel, the special chosen people of God, but she followed them anyway. She was

very humble, and left everything she had known to take care of Naomi. Like Rahab, Ruth served God and His people, and was rewarded by becoming a part of Christ's royal line. When Jesus comes to us, He will come to the people of Israel first, but then He opens His arms to include all of the nations. God does not love only the Israelites, but He loves everyone. Both the Gentiles (those people born to other nations instead of Israel) and the Israelites are saved by Jesus, and are invited into the Holy Church.

Scripture references: *Ruth, chapters 1 through 4*

The Young Prophet Samuel

There was a woman named Hannah who was terribly sad because she had no children. She prayed to the Lord God saying, "O Lord, my God of Sabaoth, look with favor upon the lowly state of Your handmaiden and remember me. I pray You, give me a son, and I will dedicate him before You as a gift until the day of his death."

Her prayers were answered: the Lord did remember her, and He sent her a son, and she called him Samuel. Just as she had promised, when her son was old enough to go serve the priests, she brought him to the temple at Shiloh, and he served Eli the priest.

One evening, Eli was lying down for bed, and his eyes were starting to grow heavy. Samuel was asleep in the temple where the ark of the covenant was, and the Lord called, "Samuel, Samuel." Samuel ran to Eli and said, "Here I am, for you called me." And Eli said, "I did not call you. Return and lie down." So he returned and lay down.

Then the Lord called again, "Samuel, Samuel!" So Samuel went to Eli a second time, and said, "Here I am, for you called me." Eli answered, "I did not call you. Return and lie down."

The Lord called Samuel again a third time. Then he arose and went to Eli, and said, "Here I am, for you called me." Then Eli realized that God was calling the boy. He said, "Return, lie down, my child; and if He calls you, you must say, 'O Lord, speak, for Your servant hears.'" So Samuel went and fell asleep again.

And the Lord came, and stood and called as before. So Samuel answered, "Speak, for Your servant hears." Then the Lord said to Samuel, "Behold! I have already told Eli that I will judge his house forever for the sinfulness of his sons. For his sons reviled God, and he did not correct them in any way."

So Samuel fell asleep and rose early in the morning. He opened the doors of the Lord's house. But Samuel was afraid to tell Eli the vision.

Then Eli called to Samuel, "Samuel, my child!" And he answered, "Here I am." And Eli said, "What did the Lord say to you? Please do not hide it from me." Samuel was afraid to tell him that Lord was unhappy with his family, but Eli explained that he was supposed to tell him. That's part of the job of the prophet. So Samuel told him everything the Lord had said, and hid nothing from him. And Eli understood and was not angry. He said, "He is the Lord. He will do what seems good to Him."

So Samuel grew and matured, and the Lord was with him. And all Israel knew that Samuel was a faithful prophet of the Lord.

Questions:

Why did Samuel's mother dedicate him to the Lord? She had no children, so she asked the Lord to send her a son and promised in return to dedicate him to the service of God.

A voice kept calling out 'Samuel! Samuel!'. Who did Samuel think it was, but who was it really? Samuel thought that Eli was calling him, but really it was God calling him.

What did God tell Samuel about Eli's family? The Lord explained to Samuel that Eli's sons had reviled the Lord and Eli had done nothing to correct them, so Eli and his family did not find favor with the Lord.

Advanced Discussion Idea:

All of Israel recognized that Samuel was the prophet of the Lord, which means that God would speak to him. Of course, the very first thing God tells him is the unpleasant news that Eli's family will be judged forever on the sinfulness of his sons. God's prophets are very special, and they are lucky to be able to talk with God, but the message God sends is not always easy to hear or easy to pass along to others.

Scripture references:
1 Kingdoms chapters 1 through 3

The Anointing of David

*G*od chose a new king for Israel, and He sent His prophet Samuel to anoint him. This means that Samuel should go and pour oil on his head and say the special blessings to mark him as God's choice for the future king. God said to Samuel, "Fill your horn with olive oil and come. I will send you to Jesse in Bethlehem, for I have seen someone among his sons to reign for Me."

When Samuel saw Jesse's sons, he looked at the oldest, who was very big and strong and whose name was Eliab, and he thought he would be God's choice for the king. But the Lord said to Samuel, "Do not be interested in his outward appearance, nor for his physical size and strength, because I have refused him. Man does not see as God sees; for man looks at the outward appearance, but the Lord sees into the heart."

So Jesse brought out each of his sons, one at a time, and made each of them pass before Samuel. And each time Samuel said, "The Lord did not choose this one either."

Then Samuel said to Jesse, "Don't you have any more sons?" Jesse said, "The only other one is the youngest, and he's out keeping the sheep." And Samuel said to Jesse, "Send and bring him. For we will not sit down till he comes here."

So he sent and brought him in. Now he was ruddy, with bright eyes, and good-looking to the Lord. And the Lord said to Samuel, "Arise, anoint David; for he is good!"

Then Samuel took the horn of olive oil and anointed him in the midst of his brothers; and the Spirit of the Lord came upon David from that day forward.

Questions:

Why does God want Samuel to pour oil on someone's head? He is anointing the person who will be the next king of Israel.

Samuel thought that Eliab, the oldest and biggest of Jesse's sons, would be God's choice for king. Why wasn't he? Because God is not interested in a person's outward appearance, their size or their strength. He is only interested in their heart.

When we hear that David was 'good-looking to the Lord' what does that mean? It must mean that when God saw into his heart, it was good; David has a good heart.

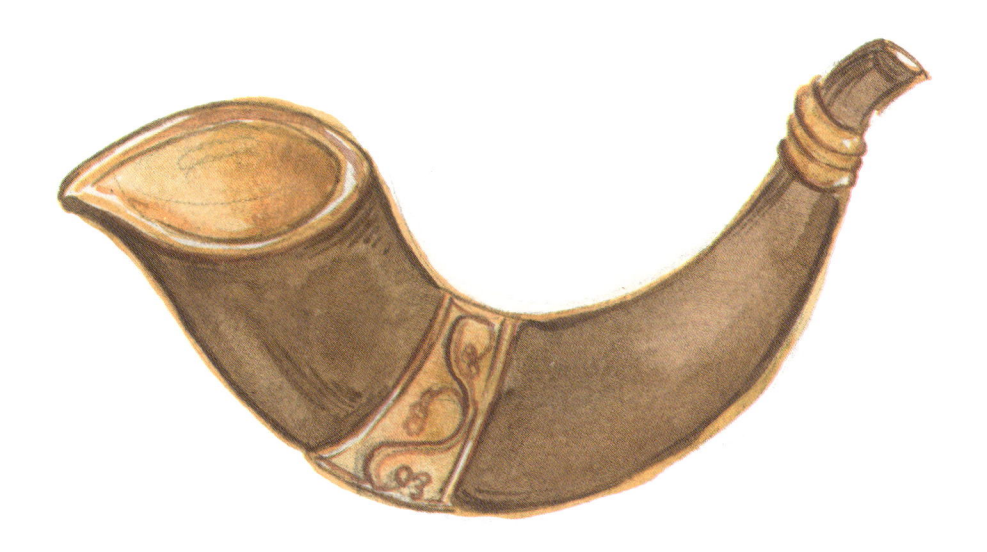

Advanced Discussion Idea:

God explained to Samuel that He sees people's hearts, and that He is not interested in the outer appearance of man. Sometimes, we look at people and we see the outside: how strong or weak they look, how smart they are, how powerful or popular they might be. But when God looks at us, He doesn't think about us in those ways. Those are earthly ways to see people. In the Kingdom of God, it is the heart that matters most.

When God sends His Son to us, He will show us the same thing: this king will not look like an earthly king, with money and palaces and power, but instead He will be born in a humble manger.

Scripture references: *1 Kingdoms 16:1-13*

David and Goliath

It was a time of war. The Philistines gathered their armies and lined up on one mountain, and the armies of Israel lined up across on another mountain, with a valley between them.

A mighty man came out from the Philistine battle line. His name was Goliath and he was nearly seven feet tall, wearing a helmet and a heavy breastplate of chain mail; he had armor made of bronze on his legs and a bronze shield between his shoulders. He was huge and terrifying, and he shouted out to the armies of Israel: "Choose a man to fight me! If he is able to kill me, then we will be your servants. But if I am able to kill him, then you shall be our servants. I challenge the ranks of the armies of Israel. Send down a man so that we can fight one on one."

When the armies of Israel heard these words, they were greatly afraid.

But from the day of his anointing, the spirit of the Lord was with David, and so even though he was younger and smaller than the others, he said, "I will go and fight with this foreigner."

Saul was leading the army, and he thought David was too young and inexperienced to fight Goliath, who was a very skilled warrior. But David said, "I used to tend the sheep for my father, and when a lion or a bear came and took a sheep out of the flock, I followed it and hit it, and saved the sheep from its mouth. And when it rose up against me, I caught it by its throat and killed it. I killed both the lion and the bear; and this man will be like one of them. Who is this Philistine who challenged the ranks of the armies of Israel? The Lord delivered me from the lion and the bear, and He will deliver me from the hand of Goliath."

So Saul said to David, "Go, and the Lord will be with you!" and he clothed David with armor, and put a bronze helmet on his head, and girded David with his sword over his armor. David tried to walk around wearing all of that armor, and then he said, "I cannot move with these, for I am not used to them." So they took them off, and he stood in his simple shepherd clothes.

Then David took his staff in his hand, and chose five smooth stones from the brook. He put them in a shepherd's bag to store away, and in his hand was his sling. Without armor, he approached the Philistine.

When Goliath saw David, he disdained him; for he was a young boy, ruddy with a good countenance. He said to David, "Am I a dog, that you come against me with a staff and stones?" Then David said, "No, you are worse than a dog!" And the Philistine cursed David by his gods.

Then David said to the Philistine, "You come to me with a sword, a spear and a shield. But I come to you in the name of the Lord Sabaoth, the God of the armies of Israel. Today the Lord will help me kill you and take your head from you. Then everyone here will know that the Lord does not save with sword and spear; for the battle is the Lord's, and the Lord will deliver you into our hands."

And the Philistine arose and moved toward David. Then David put his hand in his bag and took out one stone. He slung it and struck the Philistine on the forehead. The stone penetrated through his helmet and into his forehead. He fell to the ground on his face.

David ran and stood over Goliath, took his sword, and cut off his head to kill him. And the Philistines saw that their champion was dead, and they ran.

Questions:

When Goliath challenged the Israelites, no one wanted to fight him except David. Why? Everyone was scared of Goliath, but David trusted that God would help him defeat Goliath.

What battle experience did David have? David had never fought in a regular battle, but he had fought off a lion and a bear when he was a shepherd; he trusted that God helped him then, and He'd help him now.

David said that when he won, everyone would know that the 'Lord does not save with sword and shield'. What does that mean? David was much smaller than Goliath, and he didn't have a big sword or a fancy shield. Because of this, everyone watching will know that David didn't win because he had fancy battle gear or because of his own strength; it can only be that God made him win. God is truly the one in charge of everything.

Advanced Discussion Idea:

David did not fight for his own glory, but for the glory of God. If had he been bigger or stronger, his defeat of the giant would not have been as amazing. It is precisely because David was small and used the unsophisticated weapons of a simple shepherd, that everyone who saw knew that it truly was God's strength that defeated Goliath; through the Prophet David's own weakness, God's glory shone forth.

Scripture references: *1 Kingdoms 17*

David the Psalmist

King David was a good king, but he was not perfect. Once, he fell in love with a beautiful woman who was already married to one of his soldiers – a good man named Uriah. King David sent Uriah into a very dangerous battle on purpose, so that he would die, leaving his wife all alone, so that King David could have her.

David did not even understand that what he had done was a bad thing. God had to send another prophet, Nathan, to convince him to repent. Nathan told him a story:

There was rich man and a poor man. The rich man had many flocks and herds of animals, but the poor man had just one lamb. He raised the lamb since it was a baby, and it was his sweet pet — he fed the lamb and cuddled with the lamb and loved it very much. One day a traveler came to visit, so the rich man ordered his servants to prepare a feast. He did not want to use any of his flocks and herds, so the rich man took the poor man's lamb and served it at the feast.

King David thought this was a terrible story, and said that the rich man was cruel to the poor man. And then Nathan said that the story was really about David: King David was powerful and could marry any woman he wanted, but Uriah was just a soldier and loved his wife very dearly. When King David killed poor Uriah to take the one person he loved the most, he had committed a terrible sin.

When King David realized that Nathan's story was really his own story, and that he was the cruel man, he felt terrible. He repented his bad behavior, and God forgave him. In his lifetime, King David felt many deep emotions: he was so sad when he had done the wrong thing, and he felt grateful for God's mercy; at other times he felt love, and sometimes he was even betrayed by people he loved. Many things happened in David's life. He went to war and battled. But through all of it, he prayed.

King David was a wonderful writer, and all of his life experiences allowed him to write beautiful Psalms that sing about every part of life. Some Psalms celebrate God's creation and praise Him, and others sing about the dark Pit of sinful misery and how God's mercy is endless. It has been said that there is no human emotion or experience that is not already contained in the Psalms. (David even wrote a Psalm about killing Goliath! It's number 151.) Many of the Psalms offer prophecies about Jesus – and in fact, Jesus prayed the Psalms, and we pray them too, in all of the divine services of our Holy Church.

Shout aloud to the Lord, all the earth; Serve the Lord with gladness; Come before Him with great joy. Know this: the Lord, He is God; He made us, and not we ourselves; We are His people and the sheep of His pasture. Enter into His gates with thanksgiving And into His courts with hymns; Give thanks to Him; praise His name; For the Lord is good; His mercy is everlasting, And His truth is from generation to generation. (Psalm 99).

Questions:

Why did King David send Uriah into battle, hoping he would die? Because King David wanted to have his beautiful wife for himself.

The prophet Nathan told him a story about a cruel rich man who killed a poor man's beloved lamb. Who was King David supposed to be like in this story? King David was like the cruel rich man who took the poor man's lamb.

When King David understood that Nathan was explaining that he was being cruel, how did he feel? What did he do? King David felt terrible. He repented and asked God to forgive him.

Advanced Discussion Idea:

God actually used David's weakness to teach us. When he fought Goliath, the fact that David was small and weak showed us that God must have helped him win. Later in his life, David's other weakness, his sinfulness, enabled him to teach us how to repent; he wrote beautiful Psalms about repentance, and we even pray them today. Being weak is actually part of what made David such a great prophet.

The prophets reveal God to us, but they are not perfect. Sometimes, God uses our weakness to reveal His glory.

Scripture references:
2 Kingdoms, chapters 11 and 12; Psalm 99

PROPHET DAVID

King Solomon the Wise

After King David ruled Israel for many years, his son Solomon became the next king.

One night, the Lord appeared to Solomon in a dream and said, "Make a request for yourself."

Solomon answered, "O Lord my God, I do not know how to be a good king over Your great people who cannot be numbered. Give me an understanding heart to judge Your people, to discern between good and evil. Give me wisdom."

The Lord was pleased and said, "Because you have not asked for long life nor for riches, but have asked for wisdom to be a good judge — behold, I give you an understanding and wise heart. I also give you what you did not ask—both riches and honor—so there has been no man like you among kings."

Solomon was a very wise judge, and there is a famous example of two women who came before him: they both claimed to be the mother of a newborn baby boy. The two women lived together in one house, and each had a baby boy the same week.

One woman said, "O my lord, this woman's son died in the middle of the night, so she switched our babies, and is pretending that the living baby is hers, but he is really mine." The other woman said that the living baby was really hers.

The king said, "Bring me a sword." His servants brought a sword, and then King Solomon said, "Divide the child in two, and give half to this woman and half to the other."

One woman cried out, "My lord, don't kill him! Give her the baby." But the other said, "Yes, cut him in two, so that neither of us can have him."

So the king said, "Give the child to the one who said, 'Don't kill him.' She is his mother."

All of the people agreed that King Solomon's solution was very wise indeed.

Questions:

God invited Solomon to ask him for something. What did Solomon wish for? Solomon asked for wisdom, so that he could be a good ruler for Israel.

Why was God pleased by his request? God was happy that Solomon did not ask for something selfish, like long life or riches.

How did Solomon know which woman was really the baby's mother? The real mother loved her son and would not allow him to be killed, even if that meant that someone else would raise him. The other woman would allow him to be killed, which meant that she did not truly love him.

Advanced Discussion Idea:

Solomon had the opportunity to ask for absolutely anything, and asked only for the wisdom to be a good judge and king for God's chosen people. Solomon wanted only to serve the people better – and because his request was so selfless, God granted it and gave him even more, including riches and fame. As we see in the case of the two mothers, Solomon showed great wisdom as a judge. In fact, his wisdom was so great that he is said to have written 3,000 proverbs and 1,005 songs – and three books of the Bible (Proverbs, Ecclesiastes and Song of Solomon) plus two of the Psalms.

Scripture references: *3 Kingdoms 3:4-27*

THE SONG OF SONGS

King Solomon's Reign

As King, Solomon did many great things with the wealth God had given him. He built wonderful buildings, so that Jerusalem became a beautiful city. Most importantly, he built the great Temple of Jerusalem. Seventy thousand workers plus eighty thousand stonecutters all worked together to build the enormous and wonderful Temple. In the center, as God commanded, was the holiest of holies, which is like the altar in our churches: it was a very special place, which held the Ark of the Covenant. It was decorated with giant golden cherubim, whose wings reached up to the ceiling.

When the Temple was complete, all of Israel came, and King Solomon lead them in many sacrifices and prayers. The priests brought the Ark, with the ten commandments and the manna that God fed them when they were in the wilderness, to place it in the holiest of holies, under the golden cherubim. Suddenly, the holiest of holies was filled with a great cloud – God came to them as a cloud, just as He had lead them from Egypt as a pillar of cloud, and just as He appeared as a cloud on the mountain with Moses. This cloud of God's glory filled the whole Temple.

The Lord appeared to Solomon again, and said, "I heard your prayers to make this Temple truly My house, and My eyes and My heart will be there all the days. Now if you follow me as your father David did, heeding my commandments, then I will establish your family as the kings of Israel forever. I will keep the promises I made to your father, David. But if you or your sons turn away from Me and go to serve other gods and worship them, then the kingdom will be lost." God told him, "When people ask why the Lord gave up on Israel, they will answer, 'Because they abandoned the Lord their God, who brought their fathers out of the land of Egypt, and they embraced other gods and worshiped and served them.'"

Although the Lord was very clear, Solomon and his sons did eventually worship other gods. You see, Solomon was a king with many wives, which was normal at that time. But many of Solomon's wives were not from Israel and did not worship the Lord. He married women from foreign places, like the daughter of Egypt's Pharaoh, and other princesses of faraway lands who worshipped other gods. The Law said that you could only marry a woman if she left her false religion like Ruth did, and worshipped the God of Abraham, Isaac and Israel instead of worshipping false gods, but Solomon married women who had not abandoned their gods. He even built his wives temples to those gods, and sometimes he worshipped in those temples with them.

Solomon did not fully follow the Lord like his father David had, even after the Lord appeared to Solomon twice, and gave him wonderful gifts of wisdom and riches, and specifically told him not to worship other gods.

So the Lord said, "Because you did not keep My commandments, your family cannot stay on the throne of Israel. Because I love your father David, I will wait until you die, but then I will tear the kingdom away from your son. I will not tear away the whole kingdom; the kingdom will split in two, and part will be ruled by your sons, and part will not."

And after King Solomon died, the twelve tribes of Israel split up: the tribes of Judah and Benjamin split off to become a nation called Judea, and the other ten tribes stayed in Israel where they would have many bad kings who worshipped false gods and did not follow God's commandments.

Questions:

When the Israelites built the Temple, they included a space called the holiest of holies, which is like the altar in our churches. What did they keep in the holiest of holies? The Ark of the Covenant was kept in the holiest of holies, (and in it were the two tablets with the Ten Commandments, as well as manna from the wilderness.)

When the Israelites placed the Ark inside the holiest of holies, how did God show Himself and His presence there? God appeared as a cloud and filled up the whole Temple with His holy presence.

Solomon married women who worshipped different gods, and eventually he worshipped them too. God warned him that something would happen if he did this. What was it? Because Solomon was worshipping false gods, his family would not rule Israel forever. Instead, the tribes split up: two tribes became Judea, and the other ten were Israel. Israel lived under many bad kings for many years.

Advanced Discussion Idea:

The people of Israel would learn again and again the same lesson that Moses tried to teach them: if we listen to God and trust Him, doing what He says to do, everything goes well; but if we do not listen to God and follow His ways, then life becomes difficult. Even though Solomon was wise in many ways, he was not wise enough to keep his eyes on God. He chose to marry women who worshipped other gods, and soon he too was worshipping false idols and going astray; his whole family, his sons and the generations that came after them, would all wander around, worshipping other gods and forgetting the God of Israel who loved them.

Scripture references:
3 Kingdoms, chapter 6 through 11

The Prophet Elias

In the years after King Solomon, Israel had many bad kings and they worshipped false gods and lead the people astray. One such king was Ahab. He and his wife, Jezebel, worshipped the false god Baal, and they encouraged the people of Israel to do the same.

God sent the prophet Elias to say to the people: "You must make a choice. If the Lord is God, follow Him, but if Baal is the real god, then follow him. You cannot follow both." But the people did not answer, so Elias said, "I am the only prophet of the Lord here, but there are four hundred and fifty men who are prophets of Baal. Let's try this: bring us two oxen. Let Baal's men choose one bull for themselves, and set it up to be roasted over wood; but they shall not light a fire under it. I will prepare the other bull and lay it on the wood; and I will not light a fire under it. Then they can call their gods, and I will call on the name of the Lord, my God. Whichever God answers by lighting the fire is the true God."

The people thought this was a good test, so they agreed.

The prophets of Baal prepared their ox and their firewood, and then they called out all morning, "Hear us, O Baal, hear us." But Baal did not answer, and no matter what they did, Baal did not light that fire because Baal is not a real god.

Finally, at the end of the day, Elias stood up to take his turn. With twelve stones for the twelve tribes of Israel, he built an altar to the Lord. He piled up the firewood under his ox, and said, "Bring me four pots of water, and pour it on the firewood." They did. Elias asked them to do it a second time and a third time – twelve pots of water were poured all over that firewood, making it very wet – and of course, wood does not burn when it's wet! The whole altar was wet and the water puddled on the ground.

Then Elias cried out, "O Lord God of Abraham, Isaac, and Israel, answer me, O Lord, answer me with fire, and let the people know You are the Lord God." Immediately, the Lord sent fire from heaven and burnt up the meat offering, the firewood, and even the water. It was amazing! The people said, "Truly, the Lord is God!"

But King Ahab's wife Jezebel was angry that Elias embarrassed her false god, Baal. She threatened to kill him, but he escaped into the wilderness, to hide. He prayed and prayed, and then, exhausted, he fell asleep under a tree.

As he slept, someone touched him and said, "Arise and eat." It was the angel of the Lord! He gave him a little cake and some water, so Elias drank and went back to sleep. The angel of the Lord came back a second time, and said, "Arise and eat, because the journey is a great many days for you." So he woke up and ate and drank; and that special food kept him strong for forty days and forty nights of journeying, until he went into a cave and rested.

The Word of the Lord came to him and told him, "Go out tomorrow and stand on the mountain; and behold, the Lord will pass by. But first a great and powerful wind will be rending the mountains and shattering the rocks; but the Lord will not be in the wind. After the wind, there will be an earthquake, but the Lord will not be in the earthquake. After the earthquake, there will be a fire, but the Lord will not be in the fire.

After the fire, there will be a sound of a gentle breeze, and the Lord will be there."

Questions:

The prophets of Baal called and called out to their god, but he did not light the fire. What did Elias do to make his fire even harder to start? Why? Elias asked the people to pour four pots of water over his firewood, three times. This made the wood very wet, so that it would not burn. He did this so that people would know that God must have helped him, because only a miracle would light that wet wood on fire.

To escape Jezebel's wrath, Elias fled to the wilderness. How did he receive food, and how long did it last? The angel of the Lord brought him cakes and water twice – and those two meals were enough to fuel him for forty days as he journeyed.

There was a great and powerful wind, and then an earthquake and then a fire, but God was not in any of these. Where was God? God was in the gentle breeze.

Advanced Discussion Idea:

The Prophet Elias was allowed to witness God Himself, but first, God showed him a strong wind and then an earthquake and finally a huge fire – and then after showing him all of those powerful forces, He showed Himself to be in the gentle breeze. God's presence is sometimes so subtle that we might miss it.

After showing the people of Israel that only God could be the One True God, as He lit the fire when Baal did not, the nation of Israel would continue to follow Jezebel and Baal.

Elias saw that God's power does not always change human hearts, for God does not behave like an irresistible force – truly, He is a gentle breeze, and He allows us to use our free will to choose whether we will follow Him or not. He does not force us to love Him.

Scripture references: *3 Kingdoms 18:20-19:12*

The Chariot of Fire

God told Elias to go find Elisha, because he would be the next prophet of God, to follow Elias when he died. So he went out and found Elisha, who was plowing with twelve yoke of oxen before him. Elias threw his mantle (which is like a cloak or a coat) on him, and Elisha understood that he was being called to become a prophet.

Elisha left his family and everything he had, and he followed Elias. For some time he walked with Elias, learning from the wise prophet but also being good company for him. Eventually, God let the prophets know that it was time for Elias to go. But unlike most people, Elias would not die a normal death; instead God would come and take him up in a whirlwind, without him actually dying!

On the day when the whirlwind was supposed to come, Elias and Elisha were walking. Elias turned to Elisha and said, "Stay here, please, for the Lord sent me to Bethel." But Elisha said, "As the Lord lives, and as your soul lives, I will not leave you!" So they went to Bethel.

When they were in Bethel, the sons of the prophets there said to Elisha, "Do you know today is the day the Lord will take up Prophet Elias?" And he said, "I know. Please keep silent!"

Then Elias said to him, "Elisha, stay here, please, for the Lord sent me to Jericho." But Elisha said, "As the Lord lives, and as your soul lives, I will not leave you!" And they went to Jericho.

When they were in Jericho, the sons of the prophets there said to Elisha, "Do you know today is the day the Lord will take up Prophet Elias?" And he said, "I know. Please keep silent!"

Then Elias said to him, "Stay here, please, for the Lord sent me on to the River Jordan." But Elisha said, "As the Lord lives, and as your soul lives, I will not leave you!" So both of them went to the River Jordan.

Fifty men of the sons of the prophets went and stood at a distance, looking at them.

Elias took his mantle, rolled it up, and hit the river. The water divided this way and that, and the two of them crossed on dry ground. As they were crossing, Elias said to Elisha, "Ask me for what you would like, before I am taken away." Elisha said, "Please let me have a double portion of your grace." Elias answered, "You have asked a hard thing. If you see me when I am taken up, it shall be so, but if not, it shall not be so."

As they walked and continued to talk – behold! A chariot of fire appeared with horses of fire, and the fire separated them one from the other; and Elias was taken up into heaven by a whirlwind – and his mantle dropped down to Elisha.

Elisha saw it and cried aloud, "Father, O father, the chariot of Israel and its horsemen!"

He saw Elias no more. He put on Elias' mantle, and stood on the bank of the River Jordan. He tried to hit the water with the mantle like Elias had done, but it did not divide. Then he said, "Where is the Lord God of Elias?" And he struck the water again, and this time, it divided, and Elisha crossed over.

ST PROPHET ELIAS

Questions:

Elias kept telling Elisha to stay behind, but Elisha kept insisting that he would stay with Elias. Why? What was supposed to happen? All of the prophets understood that today was the day when God would take Elias up in a whirlwind. Elisha would not leave his friend, but stayed with him until the end.

Did Elias die and go to heaven? No – instead, God took him up while he was still alive. A chariot of fire came down and took him up in a whirlwind.

Did Elisha receive the same grace, the same prophetic power, that Elias had? Yes – he received double the grace Elias had.

Advanced Discussion Idea:

The Prophet Elias did not die, but was taken up into heaven in a whirlwind. Only one other person in the Scriptures does not die: Noah's great-grandfather Enoch, "was well-pleasing to God" and he did not die, but instead God just took him to heaven. (Genesis 5:24). The Scriptures say that two 'witnesses' will come back at the end of time, and they will be God's prophets who teach all of the people. (Revelations 11:3-4). The Church Fathers teach that these two witnesses are Enoch and Elias, who went to heaven without ever dying.

Scripture references:
3 Kingdoms 19:13-21 and 4 Kingdoms, chapter 2

The Prophet Elisha

Before the prophet Elias was taken up in a whirlwind, Elisha asked if he could have a double portion of the grace of Elias, and because Elisha was there with him when he was taken up, he did receive it. God gave him so much grace that he was able to perform many miracles.

Once, a man died owing some money, and his widowed wife came to Elisha, crying, "My husband owed money, and now they will take my two sons as slaves to pay his debt." Elisha wanted to help her, so he asked, "What do you have in the house?" She replied, "I have nothing but a small amount of oil I use to anoint myself." So Elisha told her to gather every container she could find, all of her own plus any she could borrow from her neighbors. He said to go inside her home with them, and shut the door, so that just she and her sons and all of the empty containers were inside. Then they should start pouring her little bit of oil into those containers. She and her sons found that the oil poured and poured and kept pouring until all of those containers were full! They were able to sell the oil, using the money to pay the husband's debt and to support themselves for many years.

Another time, there was an important man named Naaman, who was the commander of the Syrian army. He was a great and honorable warrior, and very powerful – but he had an illness called leprosy, which causes painful sores on the body and could not be cured. He had a young servant girl from the land of Israel, and she told them about the prophet Elisha, who could heal even his leprosy. Naaman wanted to be cured, so he traveled to find this prophet.

Naaman went with his horses and chariot and stood at the door of Elisha's house, and Elisha sent out a messenger to him, saying, "Go and bathe in the Jordan seven times, and your flesh shall be restored to you, and you shall be clean." Now Naaman was a powerful man and he expected to be treated with great respect, so he became furious, saying, "I thought Elisha would come out to greet me; that he would stand and call on the name of his God; and that he would put his hand upon me and heal the leprosy. I could wash myself in my own river and be clean!" He went away very angry.

But his servants said, "If the prophet were to tell you to do something great, would you not do it? But here the prophet said to you, 'Bathe and be clean.'" So Naaman decided to do it. He went and dipped himself seven times in the Jordan, according to Elisha's instruction, and his flesh became healthy and new like the flesh of a little child, and he was cleansed. His leprosy was gone.

Then Naaman, with all his servants, returned to Elisha and stood before him said, "Indeed, now I have come to know that in all the earth there is no God except the God of Israel. I will no longer offer burnt offering or sacrifice to other gods, but to the Lord alone." And Elisha said to Naaman, "Go in peace."

Many years later, Elisha died and was buried. The next year, some people were burying another man in the same cemetery, but a band of raiders came by, so the people quickly tossed the dead man into the prophet's tomb. When the man touched the bones of Elisha, he stood up on his feet – the grace of God still in Elisha's bones brought him back to life!

Questions:

When the widow came to Elisha and was afraid that her sons would be taken away as payment for her dead husband's debt, what miracle did Elisha do? He made her small amount of oil pour and pour to fill up many containers, so that she could sell the oil to pay off the debts.

*Naaman, the Syrian army commander who had leprosy, came to Elisha to be healed. Why didn't he like it when Elisha's servant came out and told him to bathe in the Jordan River? Because he was a powerful and important man, he expected the *prophet to receive him personally, and to lay his hands on him and heal him.*

When another body touched the bones of prophet Elisha, what miracle happened? The man came back to life.

Advanced Discussion Idea:

Prophet Elisha received a double-portion of the grace of Elias; that is to say that through the prayers of Elias and the generosity of God, Elisha was given more grace than even Elias had, and in fact he performed more miracles. Even his relics – his bones in his tomb – contained enough of God's grace to bring a dead man back to life! Grace is a real, physical thing; it's not imagined or unreal, but truly it has physical presence. Because he was filled with so much grace (a double portion of Elias' grace!) in his lifetime, that grace actually remained in his body and in his bones, and brought life to a dead man.

Scripture references:
4 Kingdoms chapters 4 and 5, 13:20-21

The Prophet Jonah Runs from God

The word of the Lord came to His prophet Jonah, saying, "Arise and go to Nineveh, the great city, and preach to them so that they repent their wickedness."

But Jonah did not want to go to Nineveh; he did not want to preach to wicked people. So he made his own plan – he would run from the presence of the Lord. He boarded a ship for Tarshish instead of Nineveh.

But the Lord raised up a great wind upon the sea, and there was a mighty storm, and the ship was tossing on the water. It was very close to sinking. All of the sailors were afraid and they cried out to their gods – for they were all different, and worshipped many gods. They threw all of the ship's cargo into the sea, hoping to lighten the load so that it would not sink.

Jonah was down inside the ship, snoring. The sailors couldn't believe he was snoring through the storm! They woke him and told him to pray to his god. They gathered together and tried to understand who had made their god angry enough to send a storm like this. Jonah told them the truth: he was a prophet trying to escape from God. Everyone was worried that Jonah's God had sent this storm.

Jonah suggested that they throw him out to sea to save everyone else; with him off the boat, God would stop the storm. The other sailors really did not want to do that, and they cried out to the Lord and said, "Please, O Lord, do not let us die on account of this man's life, and please do not make us harm him; for you, O Lord, have brought this about." But Jonah insisted, so they threw Jonah into the sea. The storm stopped, and the sailors knew that Jonah's God was very powerful.

Jonah fell into the sea, but the Lord did not let His prophet drown. The Lord commanded a huge sea creature to swallow Jonah, and Jonah was in the belly of the sea creature three days and three nights. From the dark, dank belly of the sea creature, Jonah prayed to the Lord his God. His prayers were very beautiful, about being stuck in the dark belly of a sea creature. In fact, his prayers were prophecies about Jesus! He prayed,

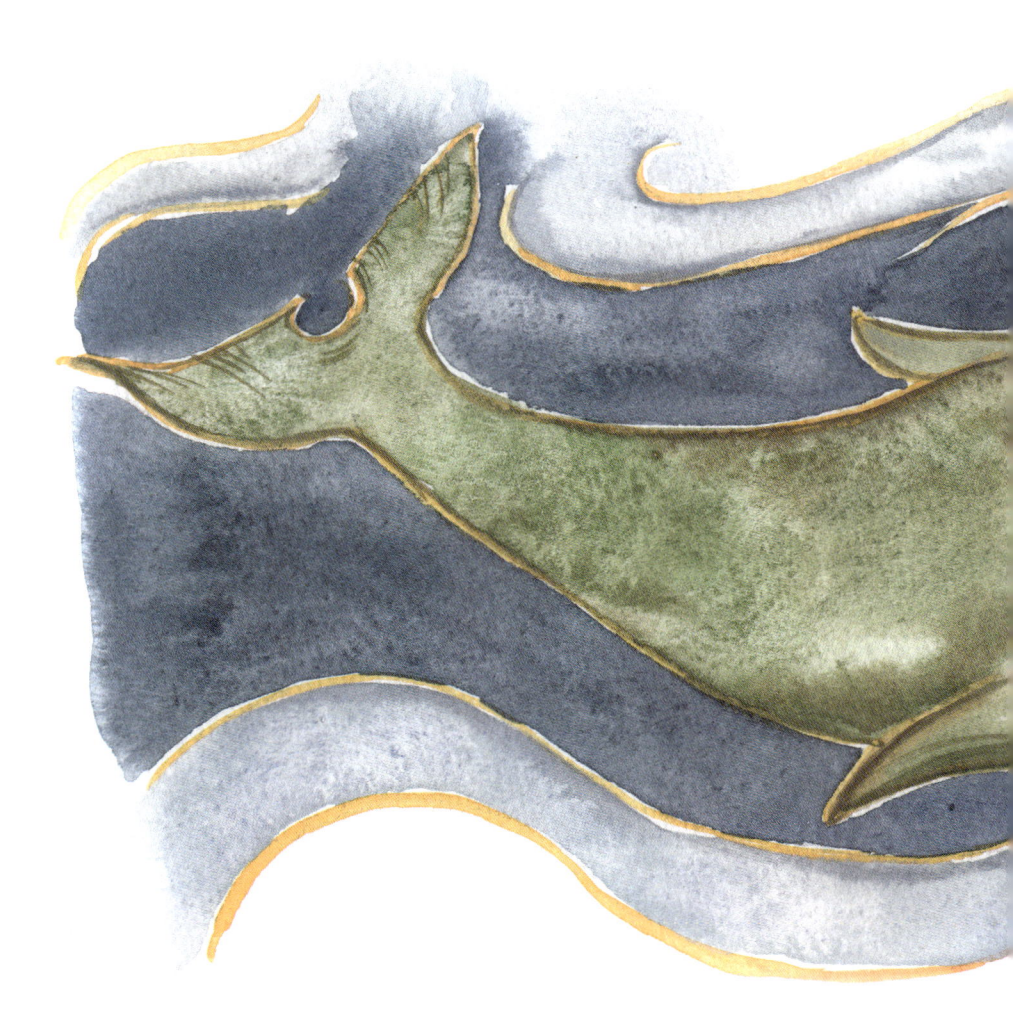

"I cried out to the Lord, my God, and He heard my voice; out of the belly of Hades, You heard the cry of my voice. You cast me into the depths of the sea. I descended into the earth, the bars of which are everlasting barriers; When my soul was failing from me, I remembered the Lord. Deliver me and save me."

Jonah was thrown into the sea and into the belly of a sea creature, but it was Jesus who descended into the earth and went into the belly of Hades. Jonah prays about Hades because he is praying about being in a dark place, but also his prayers are a prophecy about Jesus. Jonah was in the belly of the sea creature for three days, like Jesus was in Hades for three days.

After many heartfelt prayers, Jonah repented for trying to run from the presence of God, and asked for His mercy.

The Lord commanded the sea creature, and it spit up Jonah onto the dry land.

Questions:

God told Jonah to go to Nineveh, but he boarded a ship for Tarshish. Why? *Jonah did not want to preach to the Ninevites because they were wicked.*

Jonah chose to run from the presence of the Lord. Is that possible? How did God stop him from traveling to the wrong town? *You cannot run from God, because God is everywhere and sees everything. God sent down a terrible storm to stop Jonah from going to Tarshish.*

In the belly of the great sea creature, Jonah was sorry for running and prayed to God. His prayers were also a prophecy about Jesus – how was Jonah's time in the sea creature like Jesus' time in Hades? *Both Jonah and Jesus were in the dark place for three days. Jonah compared the sea creature's rib bones to the prison bars of Hades, reminding us of the gates which Jesus would break open at His Holy Resurrection.*

Advanced Discussion Idea:

The people of Nineveh were not part of God's people, Israel. They were other people, who worshipped other gods, and their wickedness was so intense that God could hear it in heaven. Imagine what this means: when God heard a wickedness so awful that its cries rose up to heaven, He reacted by sending his beloved prophet to preach there. Every human being is made in God's image, and He loves every one of us, whether we worship Him or not, whether we're good or bad or even outright wicked. He finds us lovable and He thinks it's worthwhile to try to reach out to us, even when we're being wicked.

Scripture references: *Jonah chapters 1 and 2*

The Prophet Jonah in Nineveh

Now the word of the Lord came to Jonah a second time, saying, "Arise and go to Nineveh, the great city, and preach there according to the message I previously spoke to you." This time, Jonah arose and went to Nineveh, just as he was told.

Jonah entered the city after going a day's journey, and he proclaimed, "Repent, or in three days Nineveh shall be overthrown." And the people of Nineveh believed God. They proclaimed a fast and put on sackcloth (which means that they wore rough, uncomfortable black clothes made out of goat's hair.) When the king of Nineveh heard, he arose from his throne, removed his robe, and put on sackcloth, and sat upon ashes. And it was proclaimed and spoken in Nineveh by the king and by his great men, saying, "Let not the men, cattle, oxen, or sheep taste anything, eat, or drink water." So the men and the cattle were clothed with sackcloth, and they cried out fervently to God; and they each turned back from their evil ways and from the wrongdoings of their hands, saying, "Who knows if God shall have a change of heart and turn from His fierce anger, that we should not perish?"

And God saw that they did a good job of repenting and that they turned from their evil ways. He was glad that their wickedness had ended, and He decided not to destroy the city.

But Jonah was deeply grieved and troubled; even though the people repented, he was sorry to see that God would not destroy Nineveh. He prayed, "O Lord, this is why I tried to flee to Tarshish – because I knew You would be compassionate and merciful. I wish you would destroy these people. So now, Lord, take my life from me, for it is better for me to die than to live."

And the Lord said to Jonah, "Are you upset?"

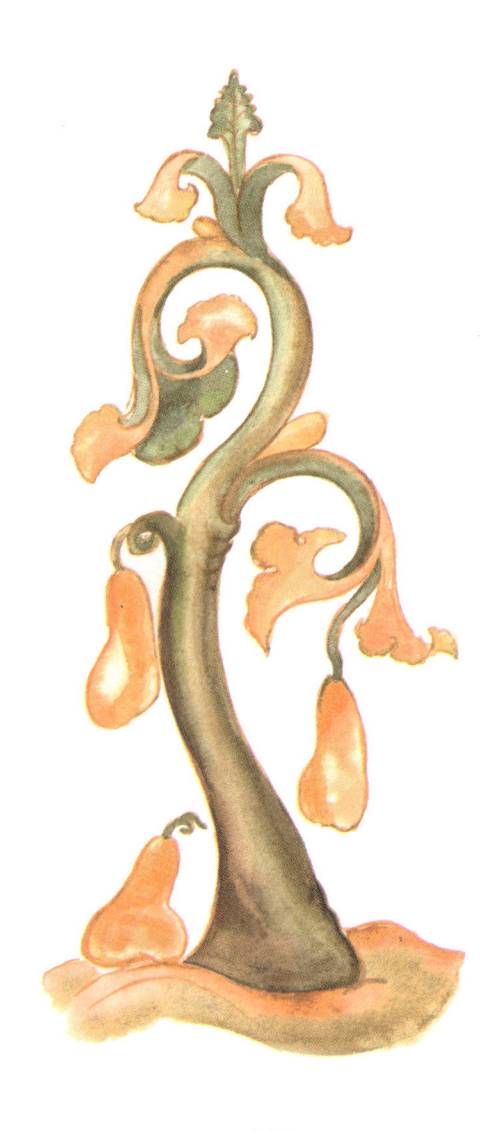

Then Jonah went out of the city and made himself a little tent on a hill, where he could sit and watch what would happen to the city. The Lord God commanded a gourd plant, and it grew quickly up over the head of Jonah to give him shade. Jonah was happy about the gourd plant.

Early the next morning, God commanded a worm, and it destroyed the gourd plant and killed it.

When the sun rose, God commanded a burning east wind; and the sun beat down on the head of Jonah, and he grew faint and despaired of his life. And he said, "It is better for me to die than to live." Then God said to Jonah, "Are you upset about the gourd?" And he said, "I am so upset that I could die." Jonah was very dramatic.

And the Lord said, "You show love and mercy for the gourd, but you did not labor for it nor did you make it grow - it just grew there one night and died the next night. Shouldn't I show love and mercy for Nineveh, the great city, with more than one hundred and twenty thousand people and all of their animals?"

But even until the end of his life, Jonah never did love Nineveh, and he wasn't glad that God loved Nineveh.

Questions:

After his experience in the belly of the sea creature, Jonah did finally go and tell the people of Nineveh to repent or God would destroy their city. What did the Ninevites do when they heard this? All of the people, including the king, immediately began to fast and to put on sackcloth, and to cry out for mercy from God. These actions showed genuine repentance for their wickedness.

When Jonah saw that the people of Nineveh listened to his prophecy and believed it, and that they did exactly what God wanted them to do, was he happy about it? What did he do? Jonah was not happy that the people repented; he wanted God to kill them all, so he was grieved that they listened and asked for God's mercy. Rather than stay among them, he went off to a nearby hill, to watch from far away.

The sun was pounding down on Jonah, so God sent him a gourd plant for shade, but then God took it away. What lesson was God trying to teach Jonah? Jonah loved that plant and wanted it to live, even though he didn't plant or raise it. God created the people of Nineveh and all of their animals, so if Jonah could love a gourd plant, shouldn't God show love for all of His creation?

Advanced Discussion Idea:

Jonah was happy to be a prophet to his own beloved Israel, but he didn't want to help God save people from other nations – especially the wicked people of Nineveh. Sometimes, we are happy to accept God's blessings, but we don't want to see God bless our enemies. But God loves all people, and there is no one so wicked that God will stop trying to reach them. Just as Jonah went into the wicked city of Nineveh, Jesus went into the darkness of Hades to preach the word of God. God will go anywhere to save us, and He works for the salvation of all sinners, everywhere.

Scripture references: *Jonah chapters 3 and 4*

Tobit and Tobias

Tobit and Anna were from Israel, but they were from one of the tribes that turned away from the One True God and worshipped Baal instead. But Tobit and Anna did not worship Baal; Tobit would walk all the way to the Temple in Jerusalem to give his offerings to God, until one day Tobit and Anna and their young son Tobias were taken captive and carried off to Nineveh.

In Nineveh, Tobit did not forget God. Even though he was a captive himself, he was very generous with all of the people he met, and tried to give away his food to the hungry ones and his clothes to those who needed clothes. Sometimes, the Ninevites would kill one of the Israelites and just throw their body over the city wall. Tobit would sneak out and find the bodies to give them a proper, dignified burial, even though he might be killed if he was caught. Once night, he was just sitting down to dinner when he heard that a young man had been killed; he ran out to steal the body at night and to give him a good burial. When he returned home very late, he fell asleep in the courtyard, and some birds pooped in his eyes; when he woke up, he had white films on his eyes and could not see well.

Tobit and Anna raised their son Tobias to love God, and to treat people with love and respect. One day, Tobit needed Tobias to journey to another city, so they hired a man to be his guide, but they didn't know that the man was really the archangel Raphael.

Tobias and the archangel Raphael went on a long journey together. When they came to the Tigris River, Tobias went down to wash himself, and a fish jumped up from the river and was determined to swallow him. The angel said, "Take hold of the fish." He grabbed the fish and put it on the bank. Then the angel said to him, "Cut open the fish. Take the heart, the liver, and the gall and put them in a safe place." Tobias did as the angel commanded and then they cooked the fish and ate it.

After this, they traveled together a while, and Tobias asked to the angel, "Why did you want me to keep the liver, the heart, and the gall of the fish?" The angel explained that they could be useful. He said, "If a demon or an evil spirit troubles anyone, the heart and the liver must be used to make smoke before the man or woman, and that person will never be troubled again. As for the gall, use it to anoint a man who has white films on his eyes, and he will be healed."

The angel told Tobias, "We will spend the night with a man who is from your tribe. He has a daughter named Sarah. She is beautiful and she is sensible, so I will speak to her father and ask if you can marry her."

Tobias said, "I have heard that she was given seven husbands, and they all died right after the wedding. Now I am my parents' only child, and I am afraid that I may die like the others. It seems that a demon is obsessed with her, and he kills anyone who tries to marry her."

But the angel told him not to worry; after the wedding, he would use the heart and liver of the fish to chase away the demon, and then he and his bride Sarah could pray to the merciful God, for His protection. Tobias agreed, and he married Sarah and sent away the demon with the smoke of the fish heart and liver. Together they prayed to God, and God kept them safe. Tobias and Sarah were happily married, and nothing bad happened to Tobias.

After a few weeks, he took his wonderful new wife home to his parents, Tobit and Anna, who were very glad to see them. Tobias used the gall from the fish to heal his father's eyesight; just as the angel promised, the white film was removed from his eyes. Finally, archangel Raphael told them who he really was all along, and the family was very grateful to the angel who guided them and taught them so much.

Questions:

Even as a captive in Nineveh, Tobit tried to help people. What kinds of things did he do? He gave his own food to people who were hungry, and gave his own clothes to people who needed them. When people died, he secretly took their bodies and gave them a proper burial.

At the river, Tobias was attacked by a fish who wanted to swallow him. What did the angel say to do? The angel told him to grab the fish and cut it open, and to keep the heart, the liver and the gall in a safe place. He said that the heart and liver would be useful to help someone who is being bothered by a demon, and the gall would heal eyes with white films on them.

Whenever Sarah would get married, her new husband would die right after the wedding. What was going wrong, and how did Tobias survive? There was a demon who was killing Sarah's husbands. The archangel Raphael taught Tobias how to make him leave with the smoke of the fish's heart and liver, and then Tobias and Sarah prayed to God for protection.

Advanced Discussion Idea:

Tobit and Tobias' whole tribe had forgotten about God. They worshipped Baal instead, and rejected God. But Tobit and Tobias, even after being captured and taken to a strange land, continued to love God. When they could no longer give their offering to the Temple, they gave it to the poor and to the people around them. Even though their tribe was lost and they were far from home, God sent an angel to guide them. He never forgets those who love Him.

Scripture references: *Tobit chapters 1 through 14*

The Prophet Isaiah

The prophet Isaiah lived 700 years before Jesus' birth, and God gave him many amazing visions. He saw the angels circling around the throne of God, and He was told many things about the Savior Jesus Christ, whom God would send to be the salvation of the world.

Isaiah told the Israelites of the tribe of David, "The Lord Himself will give you a sign: behold, the virgin shall conceive and bear a Son, and you shall call His name Emmanuel. Before the Child knows good or evil, He refuses the evil to choose the good."

Of course, he is talking about Jesus, born to the virgin Mary, and called Emmanuel, which means 'God is with us' – because when Jesus is with us, truly God is with us. Jesus never sins, but always chooses good instead of evil.

Isaiah also foretold that Jesus would come from Galilee, saying, "In the land beyond the Jordan, Galilee of the Gentiles, a people who walk in darkness, will behold a great light; and you who dwell in the country of the shadow of death, upon you a light will shine. For unto us a Child is born, unto us a Son is given. Great shall be His government, and of His peace there is no end. His peace shall be upon the throne of David and over His kingdom, to order and establish it with righteousness and judgment, from that time forward and unto ages of ages."

Isaiah foretold the birth of the Savior, who would grow up in Galilee and be a light to the gentiles and the whole world. He spoke of the coming of the wise men to offer gifts: "Herds of camels shall come to you, and the camels of Midian and

Ephah shall cover you. All those from Sheba shall come bearing gold, and they shall bring frankincense and proclaim the good news of the Lord's salvation."

God provided these clues, these prophecies about the coming of Jesus, to His prophets so that they would be ready to receive the Son of God, and so that they might recognize Him when He came. The priests and the wise men studied the prophecies, and watched and waited.

Questions:

Isaiah says that "before the Child knows good or evil, He refuses the evil to choose the good." What is he saying about Jesus? Jesus is very different from all other people, because before he even has the knowledge of good and evil, he refuses evil to choose the good. Jesus will never sin; He won't make the mistakes and the bad, selfish choices that others make, because He is perfect, because He is God.

Isaiah says that camels will come to Jesus, and that they will bring "gold, and they shall bring frankincense and proclaim the good news of the Lord's salvation." Who is he talking about? When Jesus was still just a tiny baby, only eight days old, three men from far away came with their camels to visit him. They are called the magi or the three wise men or the three kings, and they brought frankincense, myrrh and gold to honor the newborn Savior.

Why did God give so many hints about the coming of His Son? He wanted the people to know He was coming so that they would be ready for Him; they should expect Him and be prepared to follow Him. He gave them details so that they could recognize Him when He came.

Advanced Discussion Idea:

Many people expected Jesus to take over as King of Israel when He came. The prophecies talk about a Child whose "peace shall be upon the throne of David and over His kingdom, to order and establish it with righteousness and judgment." People assumed that he would reign as a very powerful earthly king. Because Herod thought this meant that Jesus might take his throne, when Jesus was born he tried to find the newborn king and kill Him. Later, the apostles would follow Jesus and teach with Him, but even they expected Him to eventually take the throne. They were surprised to realize that His Kingdom was not a kingdom on earth, but instead He reigns over the Kingdom of Heaven which is everywhere and always. The Kingdom of Heaven is eternal, unlike a simple earthly kingdom that might come and go.

Scripture references: *Isaiah 7 through 9, 11, 60*

The Prophet Ezekiel

Nebuchadnezzar was the king of Babylon, and he and his armies attacked the city of Jerusalem and took it. The soldiers plundered through the House of God, taking the beautiful chalices and vessels back to the treasure house of Nebuchadnezzar's false god. They looted the city, taking the most valuable items and the best of its people back to their homeland.

One of the people they took was the prophet Ezekiel. So many of the Israelites at that time were already worshipping Baal and other gods, and living in a foreign nation among idol-worshipping people made it even worse. But Ezekiel was a prophet of the Lord, and God did not forget him, but instead sent him many visions and messages for Israel.

Once, the word of the Lord came to Ezekiel, saying, "The house of Israel has disgraced itself, by worshipping idols and not following the Law. This is why they are scattered among the nations and living in foreign lands as captives. I do not want people to see that I did not take care of my special nation, and to think that I do not exist or that I am not the One God. For the sake of My holy name, so that all of the people will know that I am the Lord, I will gather the children of Israel and bring them home to their land. People of Israel, I shall sprinkle clean water on you, and you will be cleansed from all your idols. I shall give you a new heart and put a new spirit within you. I shall take the heart of stone from your flesh and give you a heart of flesh. I shall put My Spirit within you and cause you to walk in My commandments. You will dwell in the land I gave to your fathers. You will be My people, and I shall be your God." The people of Israel had disgraced themselves, but God would wash them clean and give them a fresh start.

The hand of the Lord came and brought Ezekiel by the Spirit of the Lord, and set him in the middle of a plain, which is like a big flat field. The plain was full of many many old dry human bones. The Lord told Ezekiel, "Prophesy to these bones and say to them, 'O dry bones, hear the word of the Lord. The Lord says to you: "Behold, I will bring the Spirit of life upon you. I will put muscles on you and bring flesh upon you. I will cover you with skin and put my Spirit into you. Then you shall live and know that I am the Lord." So Ezekiel prophesied and it came to pass that there was a shaking, and the bones came together into skeletons. And behold, muscle and flesh grew on them, and skin covered them over; but no breath was in them.

Then the Lord told Ezekiel, "Prophesy to the wind, and say Thus says the Lord: *Come from the four winds and breathe upon these dead men; and let them live.*" So Ezekiel prophesied and the Spirit entered into them; and they lived and stood upon their feet.

The Lord said, "These bones are the whole house of Israel. They say, *Our bones are dry, our hope is dead, and we are lost.* Therefore prophesy to them, Thus says the Lord: *Behold, you will know that I am the Lord, when I open your tombs to lead you, My people, up from their graves. I will put My Spirit in you, and you will live; and I will place you in your own land. Then you will know that I am the Lord. I have spoken, and I will do it.*"

Questions:

The people of Israel were scattered throughout many lands and disgraced. Why did this happen? Because the people were not following the Lord's commandments, and were worshipping false idols, so they were not all together in one nation as they would have been if they were holding together and worshipping God and following the Law.

When Ezekiel prophesied to the dry bones on the plain, what happened? There was a great shaking, and then the bones rose up *and formed skeletons, and the muscle and skin grew back on them. When Ezekiel prophesied to the wind, it blew and brought them back to life. (Just as when Jesus created human beings, and then breathed life into them.)*

What is God going to do for the nation of Israel? He is going to bring them back together, and give them new hope and new life. He will be their God, and they will be His people – following His commandments and worshipping only Him.

Advanced Discussion Idea:

Ezekiel delivers an important message to Israel and to all of us: no matter how we have disgraced ourselves, no matter how far away we've run from God, even if we feel that there is no hope and no life left in us, God can and will give us new life. With God, it is never too late. He can even bring life to old dry bones.

Scripture references:
Ezekiel chapters 36 and 37

The Prophet Daniel in Babylon

*W*hen King Nebuchadnezzar looted Jerusalem, they took more than just the Temple's beautiful chalices and treasure; they took the finest young men they could find in all of Israel, the best and the brightest of Israel's future, and educated them in their own Chaldean letters. They took all the best Israel had to offer, in order to rededicate it to their own gods and culture.

The bright young men they carried off included Daniel, Hananiah, Azariah, and Mishael. They were to be educated in Chaldean ways and to become valuable citizens of Babylon, so Nebuchadnezzar renamed them with Chaldean names: Belteshazzar, Shadrach, Meshach and Abednego.

One night, the King had a bad dream, so he called for his enchanters, magicians and sorcerers to explain it. They came right away, but the King had forgotten the dream. He insisted that they tell him what he dreamt and what it meant, but the men explained that they could only interpret the dream if the King would tell them what it was. The King argued with them, and started to think: if they were so wise, surely they could tell him what his dream was! He decided that they were fakes and frauds, and ordered that all of them be killed.

The captain of the King's guard told Daniel what was happening. He asked the King to wait before he killed them, and he went home and talked to his friends, Hananiah, Mishael, and Azariah. They all prayed to God, asking Him for the answer to this mystery of the King's dream. That night, God explained it to Daniel.

Daniel went to the King and said that his mystery cannot be revealed by enchanters, magicians and sorcerers. Only God in heaven reveals mysteries. God showed Daniel that the king saw a huge statue made of gold at the top, of silver in the middle, and then less valuable materials going down – copper, iron and clay. It was standing there, looking big and frightening but suddenly, the king saw a stone that was cut out of a mountain without hands. The stone hit the big statue on its feet and then the whole thing turned to dust and the wind blew it away. Then the stone not carved by hands became a great mountain and filled all the earth.

Daniel explained that the dream meant that God had given Nebuchadnezzar a great kingdom, and he had been a great king; that is why he was the golden head on the statue. But after him the next king would not be as good so he was silver, and the next king will be even less good so he was just copper, all the way down to the bottom of iron and clay. Then the stone cut out of the mountain without hands, which will be the King of Kings sent by God, will smash all of the other kingdoms. They will be like dust, and this great kingdom will last forever and ever. So Daniel said that the One True God had allowed the king to know what would come in the future.

Then King Nebuchadnezzar said to Daniel, "Truly, your God, He is the God of gods and the Lord of kings, who reveals mysteries, for you were able to reveal this mystery." The king exalted Daniel and gave him many great gifts. He put him in charge of Babylon and over all the wise men of Babylon, the enchanters, magicians and sorcerers. Daniel also asked the king to give important positions to Shadrach, Meshach, and Abednego and he did, but Daniel lived in the king's palace.

Questions:

What was the mystery the king needed to have solved? He had a bad dream, but could not remember it. He wanted someone to tell him what the dream was and what it meant.

Why did King Nebuchadnezzar think that all of his enchanters, magicians, and sorcerers were liars and fakes? What punishment did he choose for them? He called them to interpret his dream, but they could not tell him what the dream was; he thought that if they were not fakes, they should be able to tell him his dream. He was very angry, and ordered all them killed.

What was the king's dream and what did it mean? The king dreamed of a huge statue, with a golden head, and a body that was silver and then copper, then iron and clay at the bottom. A stone that was not cut by hands cut itself out of the mountain and destroyed the statue. The statue was King Nebuchadnezzar (the golden head) and the kings coming after him would be worse and worse, until the new King (Jesus) smashed the kingdom and established a new, eternal kingdom instead.

Advanced Discussion Idea:

The stone that was not cut by hands must have cut itself out of the large stone mountain. The false idols are always made by human beings, but the One True God is not. He may take the form of something earthly (as when He appears as a fiery cloud or when Jesus takes on a human body) but people cannot make Him as they would an idol or a statue. This great stone, the King of Kings is really Jesus Christ, coming to reign over a Kingdom that will have no end, the Kingdom of Heaven.

Scripture references: *Daniel chapter 1*

The Three Youths in the Fiery Furnace

*K*ing Nebuchadnezzar built an enormous golden statue in Babylon. At the dedication of the new statue, the herald announced the new law. He cried out in a loud voice, "When you hear the sound of the trumpet, the pipe, the harp, the four-stringed instrument, the psaltery, the symphony, and every kind of music, you shall fall down and worship the golden image King Nebuchadnezzar set up, but whoever does not fall down and worship shall be cast into the burning fiery furnace."

So whenever people heard the sound of the trumpet, the pipe, the harp, the four-stringed instrument, the psaltery, the symphony, and every kind of music, they fell down and worshipped the golden image King Nebuchadnezzar set up.

Then some of the men went to the king and said that Shadrach, Meshach, and Abednego were not worshipping the golden image with everyone else.

So Nebuchadnezzar asked them, "Is it true, Shadrach, Meshach, and Abednego, that you do not serve my gods or worship the golden image I set up? Now then, if you are ready, when you hear the sound of the trumpet, the pipe, the harp, the four-stringed instrument, the psaltery, the symphony, and every kind of music, that you shall fall down and worship the golden image I made. But if you do not worship it at that time, you shall be cast into the burning fiery furnace. Then what god is there who will deliver you from my hands?"

Shadrach, Meshach, and Abednego answered, "We have no need to answer you about this. For there is a God in the heavens, whom we serve, and He is able to save us from the burning fiery furnace; and He will deliver us from your hands, O king. But if not, let it be known to you, that we will not serve your gods, nor worship the golden image you set up."

Then Nebuchadnezzar was very angry, and he commanded them to heat the furnace seven times more, until it burned at its very hottest. And the king's men tied them up, and threw them into the burning fiery furnace – but the flames did not hurt them. The fire burned up the ropes that were tied around them, and they danced in the middle of the flames, praising the Lord. The Angel of the Lord joined them in the furnace and made it feel like a lovely breeze was blowing. The fire did not bother them at all.

Now Nebuchadnezzar heard their singing, and asked, "Didn't we cast three men into the fire? Behold, I see four men untied and walking in the midst of the fire, yet they are not destroyed; and the vision of the fourth is like the Son of God."

Then the king approached the door of the burning fiery furnace, and called out to them by name, "Shadrach, Meshach, and Abednego, servants of the Most High God, come here!" So they came out of the fire and everyone saw that they had not been harmed at all. Even their clothes were not singed, and they didn't even smell like smoke!

So King Nebuchadnezzar said, "Blessed is the God of Shadrach, Mcshach, and Abednego, who sent His Angel and saved His servants who trusted in Him!"

Questions:

What was everyone supposed to do when they heard the sound of the trumpet, the pipe, the harp, the four-stringed instrument, the psaltery, the symphony, and every kind of music? Any time they heard any music, they must fall down and worship the golden image or they shall be cast into the burning fiery furnace.

When the king's men threw them into the burning fiery furnace, with the heat turned up seven times, what happened? The fire did not harm them at all. It just burned up the ropes, so they could move around freely and praise God. The Angel of the Lord came into the furnace and made it feel like it wasn't even hot.

What did Nebuchadnezzar think when he saw the four figures in the furnace? He knew that it was a miracle that instead of three tied up men, he saw four untied men, and he recognized the fourth as the Son of God. He immediately admitted that their Most High God had saved them.

Advanced Discussion Idea:

The Son of God did not abandon His beloved youths in this strange land filled with false gods, but when they were cast into the terrible fiery furnace, He joined them there! He loved them so much, that He would go anywhere to protect them. Especially when someone is suffering, God comes to them, joining them in the difficult places.

Scripture references: *Daniel chapter 3*

The Prophet Daniel in the Lion's Den

After Nebuchadnezzar, Darius became the king. He had many governors ruling the lands, but he liked Daniel the best. Daniel was so excellent that Darius put him in charge of all the other governors and administrators. They were jealous, and they tried to find a way to get him in trouble. But as hard as they tried, they could not find any crime or wrongdoing, because Daniel was faithful and good.

But they knew that he was faithful to His God, so they decided to use that against him.

They went to the king and said, "King Darius, we have established a new decree, that whoever asks anything from any god or man, except from you, O king, shall be cast into the den of lions. Now therefore, O king, establish the decree and exhibit the writing publicly, so that the decree cannot be changed." King Darius agreed.

When Daniel heard the decree was posted, he entered his house and knelt down on his knees three times that day, praying and giving thanks to his God, as he had always done. But those men were watching, and they saw his prayers and ran to the king, saying, "did you not give orders that any man who asked anything from any god or man, except from you, would be cast into the den of lions?" The king agreed. Then they told him that Daniel had not obeyed the order, for he prayed three times daily to his God!

When the king heard their words, he was very sad. He had not meant to make Daniel's prayers a crime. He tried to change the law, but it could not be changed. He tried to argue in favor of saving Daniel, but everyone insisted. There was nothing more to say.

They took Daniel and threw him into the lions' den. But the king said to him, "Your God will deliver you." Then they brought a stone and placed it over the mouth of the den, and the king headed home, so upset that he could not eat or sleep. But in the lion's den, all was peaceful. God shut the mouths of the lions, and they did not bother Daniel at all.

The king arose early with the sunrise and hurried to the lions' den, crying out in a loud voice, "Daniel, servant of the living God, has your God been able to deliver you from the mouth of the lions?" Daniel answered, "My God sent His angel and shut the mouths of the lions so they did not destroy me, because I did no wrongdoing in His sight." The king rejoiced greatly and gave orders to bring Daniel out of the den.

Now King Darius wrote a new decree: "In every dominion of the kingdom, men must tremble and fear before the God of Daniel, because He is the living God; He endures unto the ages. His kingdom shall not be destroyed, and His dominion shall continue to the end. He helps and rescues, and works signs and wonders in heaven and on earth; for He delivered Daniel from the power of the lions."

Daniel lived a long life in Babylon, in charge of all the magi and wise men. God showed him visions of many things, including the exact year when Jesus Christ would be born. Daniel prophesied to the other magi about the birth of a new King, the Son of God who would come down in the flesh. He told them to watch for a star to lead them to the newborn king, when the time was right. They listened to their trusted, wise friend, and they waited.

Questions:

The administrators were jealous of Daniel, so they asked Darius to make a decree, secretly knowing that Daniel could not obey it. What was the decree? The decree said that whoever asks anything from any god or man, except from the king, shall be cast into the den of lions.

How did Darius react when Daniel was safe in the lions' den the next morning. Darius rejoiced, because he did not want Daniel harmed. He was impressed that Daniel's God had taken good care of him, and decreed that everyone should be respectful of his good and powerful God.

The Prophet Daniel left prophecies for the wise men of Babylon, telling them exact year of Christ's birth. What did he say would lead them to the newborn king? He said that a star would guide them to the newborn king.

Advanced Discussion Idea:

God's prophets are like a lamp to the whole world, shining the light of Christ into the darkness. Daniel fulfilled this role well, showing God's light to the Chaldeans in Babylon. He did not lecture them or argue with them, but instead he just lived a holy life. They could see how Daniel loved God and how God blessed Daniel, and they came to understand that his God was powerful and loving. We can learn from Daniel how to quietly witness to God's greatness without arguments or words.

Scripture references: *Daniel 6*

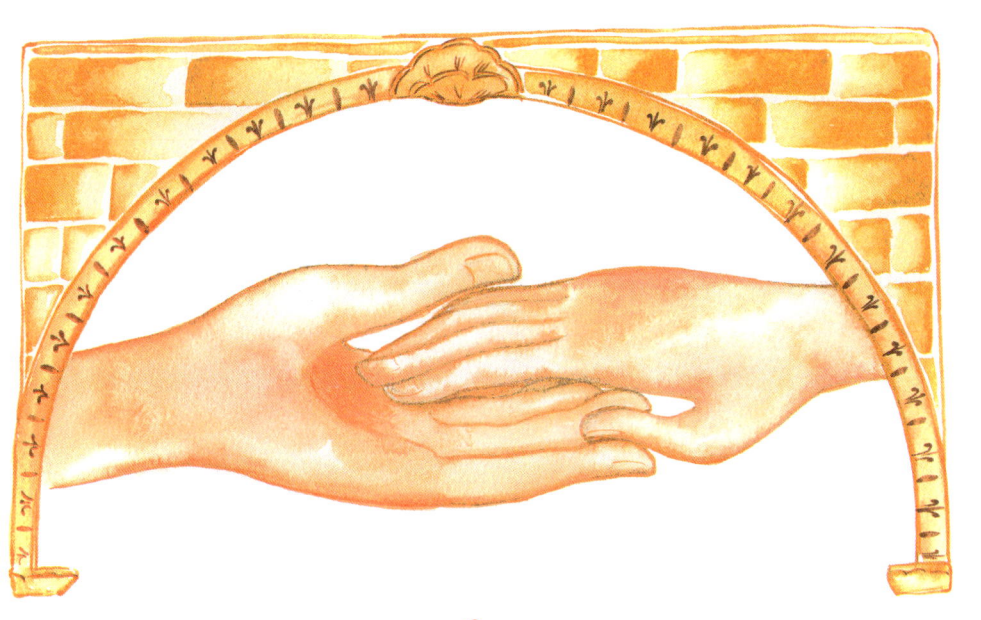

Saints Joachim and Anna

M*any years* later, when Herod was the King of Judea, there was a man named Joachim who was a wealthy shepherd in Nazareth, known for his generosity. He would add up all of his lambs and sheep, their wool and his profits, and he would give one third to the orphans, widows, strangers and the poor; he would give another third to the Temple and its servants and those who worshipped God; and he would keep only the last third for himself and his household. Because he was so generous and good, the Lord blessed him and multiplied his flocks.

When Joachim was twenty years old, he married Anna, a girl from Bethlehem. They wanted children but no children came, until finally they were very old. One day, Joachim brought his usual, generous offering to the Temple, but Zacharias, the high priest, sent him away, saying that God must be judging

Joachim by not sending children. Joachim was heartbroken. He took his sheep deep into the countryside, and pitched a tent. He would not eat or drink, but he fasted and prayed.

While Joachim was in the wilderness, Anna walked in the garden. As she prayed, she thought about Sarah, Abraham's wife who gave birth to Isaac in her very old age. She noticed a sparrow's nest on a laurel branch, and prayed to the Lord about how the birds had babies, but she did not. Like Joachim, she was very sad, so she prayed and drew closer to God.

One day, the angel Gabriel came to Joachim and said that God knew about his generosity and his love, and heard his prayers. He said, "Anna, your wife, will bring forth a daughter and you shall name her Mary. She will be devoted to the Lord from her infancy, and she shall be filled with the Holy Spirit, even from her mother's womb. Mary shall not eat or drink anything unclean, nor shall she be among the crowds of the people, but in the Temple of the Lord. She will be born to a barren woman, and then later she will give birth to the Son of the Most High, the Savior of all nations." As the angel left him, he said that Joachim would find his wife at the Golden Gate.

Meanwhile, in the garden, Anna did not know that the angel visited her husband with amazing news, and she was still very sad. Then the same angel of the Lord appeared to her, saying, "Anna, Anna, the Lord has heard your prayer, and you shall conceive a child and your seed shall be spoken of in all the world." And Anna said, "As the Lord my God lives, whether I have a boy or a girl, I will bring it as a gift to the Lord my God; and my child shall minister to Him all the days of its life." The angel told her also, to look for her husband at the Golden Gate.

Just as the angel promised, Joachim and Anna arrived at the Golden Gate at the same time, and both were filled with joy at the wondrous tidings they had heard. Anna gave birth to their daughter, and they named her Mary.

On Mary's third birthday, her parents and all of their friends had a beautiful procession, bringing Mary to the Temple, where the high priest Zacharias was waiting to receive her. She was so happy to be there that she ran up the stairs. Her uncle the high priest gave her a tour of the Temple, and because she was to be the Mother of God, he brought her into the holiest of holies. Before Mary arrived, only the high priest could enter the holiest of holies, and he would only do so one day a year, on the Day of Atonement. But Zacharias brought Mary into this holiest place, and she was frequently visited by angels there, who brought her food and talked with her. Mary grew up happily in the Temple, with a small group of other young girls, all dedicated to the service of the Lord.

Questions:

Joachim gave some of his money to the poor and some to the Temple, but how much did he keep for himself? Joachim gave one third to the poor, and one third to the Temple, and kept only one third for himself and his family.

Why did Zacharias the high priest refuse to accept Joachim's generous offering to the Temple? He thought that by not sending children to them, God was saying that Joachim and Anna were doing something bad.

The angel Gabriel visited both Joachim and Anna, bringing good news. What did he say would happen? The angel said that Joachim and Anna would have a daughter and they should name her Mary. He said that she would live in the Temple, dedicated *to God, and while she was still a virgin she would give birth to the Son of the Most High, the Savior of all nations. He also said that they would find each other at the Golden Gate.*

Advanced Discussion Idea:

The angel told Joachim that Mary was chosen to be the Mother of God. Because it was understood that she would give birth to our Lord, Zacharias allowed her to enter into the holiest of holies. This is where the Ark of the Covenant was kept, and it was very special because God was present in the Ark. Mary is like the Ark and would also become a mystical container for the One True God, so it was appropriate that she be there in that holiest place.

Reference:
The source for this section is Chapters 1 through 3, from *The Life of the Virgin Mary, the Theotokos*, written and compiled by Holy Apostles Convent, Colorado, 1989.

The High Priest Zacharias

Zacharias was the high priest of the Temple; he and his wife, Elizabeth, were both righteous before God, but they had no child, because Elizabeth was barren, and they were both very old.

Once a year, the high priest would be sent into the holiest of holies, and this year was Zacharias' turn. It was the day of Atonement, so he was to go inside and burn incense and pray for the forgiveness of everyone's sins. So while an enormous crowd of people was waiting outside the Temple, he went inside.

Suddenly an angel of the Lord appeared to him, and when Zacharias saw him, he was troubled and afraid.

But the angel said to him, "Do not be afraid, Zacharias, for your prayer is heard; and your wife Elizabeth will bear you a son, and you shall call his name John. And you will have joy and gladness, and many will rejoice at his birth. For he will be great in the sight of the Lord, and shall drink neither wine nor strong drink. He will be filled with the Holy Spirit, even while he is in his mother's womb. And he will turn many of the children of Israel to the Lord their God. He will get the people of Israel ready, prepared to receive the Lord."

Zacharias did not believe him. He argued with the angel, saying, "How shall I know this? For I am an old man, and my wife is very old."

The angel answered and said to him, "I am Gabriel, who stands in the presence of God, and was sent to speak to you and bring you these glad tidings. But behold, you will be mute and not able to speak until the day when all these things take place, because you did not believe my words."

The people waited for Zacharias, and they thought it was strange that he took so long in the Temple. But when he came out, he could not speak to them for he was now mute; and they understood that he had seen a vision in the temple, because he spoke to them in hand signals but his voice was silent.

So when the days of his service in the Temple were complete, he departed back to his own house. Soon after, his wife Elizabeth conceived a child. She prayed, grateful that the Lord had blessed her with a child so that people would no longer believe that He was judging her to be unworthy by not sending children.

But Zacharias still could not talk, because he did not believe the angel in the Temple.

Questions:

As a high priest of the Temple, Zacharias was chosen for what special job? He was chosen to go into the holiest of holies to light incense and offer prayers for the forgiveness of everyone's sins.

What news did the angel bring? He said that Zacharias and Elizabeth would have a wonderful child, who would be filled with the Holy Spirit and would call on the people of Israel to repent and prepare to receive Christ.

What punishment did Zacharias receive for not believing the angel? The angel made him mute, so that he could not speak, until the child was born and named John.

Advanced Discussion Idea:

In the Temple, Zacharias was praying for the forgiveness of his people's sins, so when the angel said, "your prayer is heard; and your wife Elizabeth will bear you a son" it was confusing; Zacharias was not praying for a baby. He did not expect that the forgiveness of Israel's sins would come through his own son, John, who would lead Israel to repentance in preparation for Jesus. Of course, even if the angel Gabriel says something unexpected, he should be believed, for he stands in the presence of God; he cannot be wrong, and nothing is impossible with God.

Scripture references: *Luke 1: 5-25*

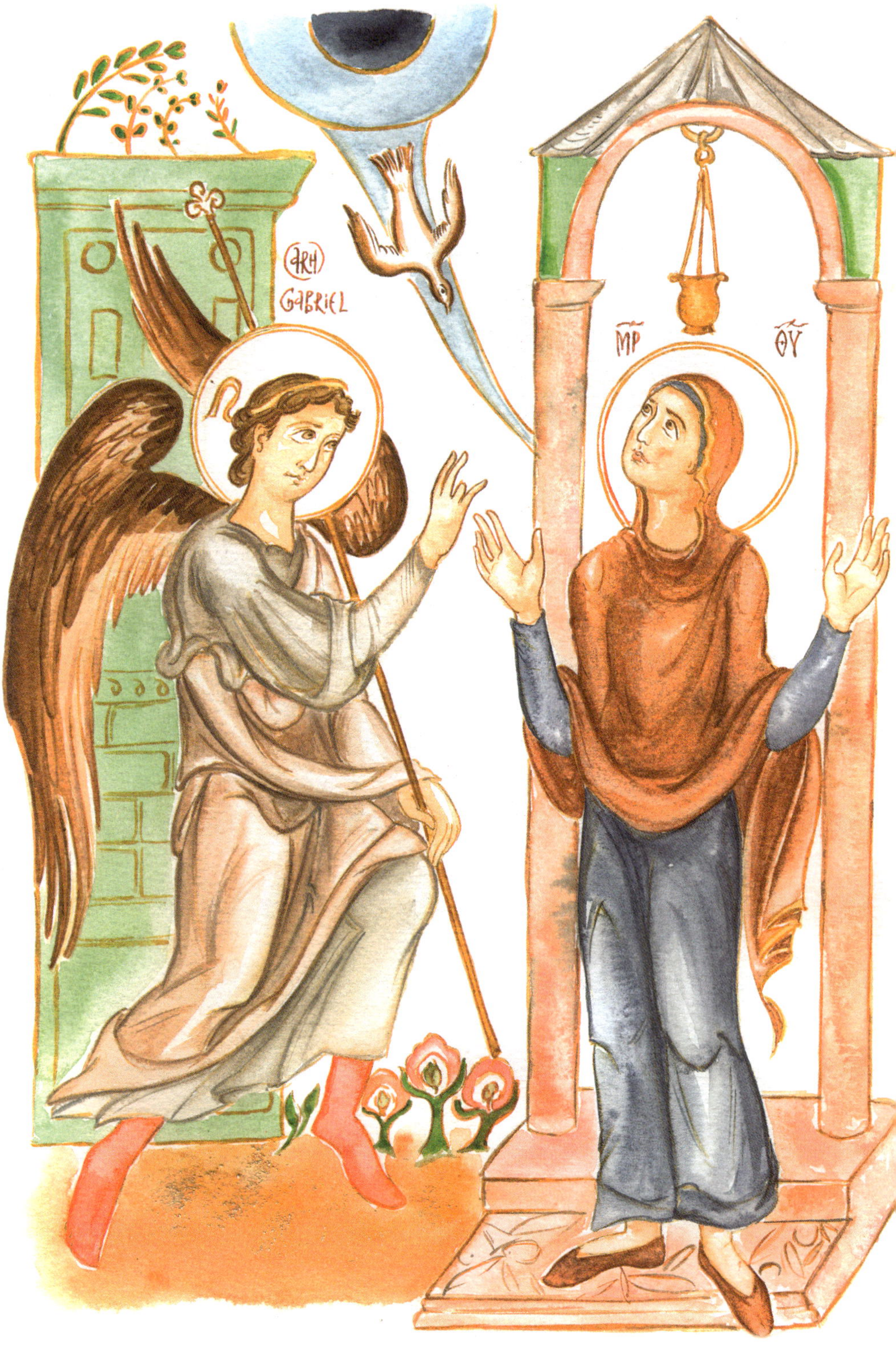
ARH
GABRIEL
MP
ΘV

The Annunciation

Mary grew up in the Temple, and her life was like a nun's life: she was in a community where everyone served the Lord, and she spent her time praying and doing handiwork, like spinning thread and weaving cloth. But in Mary's day, a woman could not simply become a nun. As a child she could live in the Temple, but as she grew into a woman, she would have to move to a household, as someone's daughter or as someone's wife. Of course, Joachim and Anna were very old when Mary was born, and by the time she grew into a young woman, they had died. Mary had no father to take care of her, so she would have to marry.

Mary did not want to be married. She wanted to live a chaste life, in prayer and service to God. Like a nun, Mary vowed to chastely serve the Lord for the rest of her life, and she refused to break that vow.

Zacharias the high priest went into the holiest of holies, and asked God what he should do with Mary. The angel Gabriel appeared, and told him that each of the old widowers in the community should come to the Temple with his rod, and that God would give a sign telling them which one should take care of Mary. So the widowers brought their rods.

Joseph of Nazareth was an eighty year old man who had been married to a good woman named Salome. She loved the Lord very much, and she and Joseph had seven children, four sons and three daughters. They lived together happily for forty years, but then she died. Joseph had been a widower for just one year when he was called to bring his rod to the Temple.

The priests placed all of the rods in the holiest of holies, and the next day, Joseph's rod had sprouted three small leaves; this was a sign from God that Joseph should take care of Mary. Joseph had grandsons older than Mary, and he was concerned that it would look ridiculous for an old man to take care of this young girl, but God had chosen him, so Joseph agreed to protect her. He would take Mary into his home, along with five of her friends, virgins from the Temple, so that she would not be lonely.

Mary and her friends continued to serve the Temple, spinning thread and weaving fabric. One day, as she was spinning purple thread that would be used to weave the new temple veil, Mary was visited by the angel Gabriel, who said, "Rejoice, the Lord is with you; blessed are you among women! Do not be afraid, Mary, for you have found favor with God. And behold, you will conceive in your womb and bring forth a Son, and shall call His name Jesus. He will be great, and will be called the Son of the Highest; and the Lord God will give Him the throne of His father David. And He will reign over the house of Jacob forever, and of His kingdom there will be no end."

Mary asked, "How can this be, since I do not know a man?" And the angel answered, "The Holy Spirit will come upon you, and the power of the Highest will overshadow you; therefore, also, that Holy One who is to be born will be called the Son of God. Now indeed, Elizabeth your relative has also conceived a son in her old age; and this is now the sixth month for her who was called barren. For with God nothing will be impossible."

Mary answered, "Behold the maidservant of the Lord! Let it be to me according to your word." And the angel departed from her.

Questions:

When a girl was no longer a child and became too old to live in the Temple, she had to go back to her father's house or get married. Why didn't Mary want to get married? Mary was like a nun; she wanted to live a chaste life and serve God with all of her energy. She yearned to dedicate herself totally to God.

Why was Joseph reluctant to become Mary's protector? Joseph was eighty years old, and had grandsons older than Mary. He was worried that it would seem ridiculous for him to be the one protecting this young virgin who had vowed to serve God forever. But because God chose him through his rod, he agreed.

When the angel Gabriel told Mary that she would be the Mother of God, how did she react? She was curious about the details, and she was obedient and happy to serve the Lord however He needed her. She did not argue or refuse, but said, "let it be to me according to your word".

Advanced Discussion Idea:

The Fathers call Mary the new Eve, because in the Garden of Eden, the first Eve disobeyed God's commandment not to eat the fruit of tree, causing mankind to fall – but Mary is like a second chance, and this woman is obedient to God's will and wishes only to do what is pleasing to God and best for mankind. Where Eve ignored God and did what she wanted, Mary does not worry about her own desires or wish to explore other ideas. Mary trusts God, and is happy to cooperate with God's will, so she says yes to the angel. The child she bears will fix the fall, and saving mankind from death and opening the gates of Paradise.

Scripture references:
Luke 1: 26-38 and Chapters 2 through 6 from
The Life of the Virgin Mary, the Theotokos,
written and compiled by Holy Apostles Convent,
Colorado, 1989.

Mary visits Elizabeth

After the angel's visit, Mary and the other young women finished spinning the purple thread for the Temple, and then traveled several days to Jerusalem to deliver it. Then they continued walking for one more day, to the hill country, to the home of the high priest Zacharias, whose wife Elizabeth was Mary's cousin. Of course, Zacharias was still mute from not believing the angel, and Elizabeth was still pregnant with their son, who would be named John.

When her cousin heard Mary's voice, the baby leaped in her womb and Elizabeth was filled with the Holy Spirit. She spoke out with a loud voice, "Blessed are you among women, and blessed is the fruit of your womb! But why is this granted to me, that the mother of my Lord should come to me? For indeed, as soon as the voice of your greeting sounded in my ears, the babe leaped in my womb for joy. Blessed is she who believed, for there will be a fulfillment of those things which were told her from the Lord." Amazingly, Elizabeth already knew that Mary was pregnant and that she believed when the angel came to her. Even more amazingly, both she and the baby in her womb, John, recognized that her baby was the Son of God. They were among the earliest Christians, because they knew their Lord even before He was born!

Mary said, "My soul magnifies the Lord, and my spirit has rejoiced in God my Savior. For He has regarded the lowly state of His maidservant; behold, all generations will call me blessed. For He who is mighty has done great things for me, and holy is His name. And His mercy is on those who fear Him from generation to generation. He has shown strength with His arm; He has scattered the proud in the imagination of their hearts. He has put down the mighty from their thrones, and exalted the lowly. He has filled the hungry with good things, and the rich He has sent away empty. He has helped His servant Israel, in remembrance of His mercy, as He spoke to our fathers, to Abraham and to his seed forever." And Mary remained with Elizabeth for about three months, and returned to Joseph's house.

After Mary left, Elizabeth's baby was ready to be delivered, and she gave birth to a son. Her neighbors and relatives rejoiced with her that God sent her a child!

On the eighth day, they came to circumcise the child and they were going to call him by his father's name, Zacharias, for that was what everyone expected. But Elizabeth said, "No; he shall be called John." They were confused, and said, "There is no one among your relatives who is called by this name." So they made signs to his father, Zacharias to see which name he preferred. Zacharias still could not speak, so he asked for a writing tablet, and wrote, "His name is John." They were all amazed.

Immediately Zacharias' mouth was opened and his tongue was loosed, and he spoke, praising God.

Then fear and amazement came on all who dwelt around them; and all these things were discussed throughout all the hill country of Judea. They knew that they were witnessing miracles. All those who heard about these things kept them in their hearts, saying to each other, "What kind of child will this be?"

And the hand of the Lord was with John.

Questions:

When Mary had just arrived and only called out to Elizabeth, her cousin already knew that she was the Mother of God. How did she know? We don't know how she knew. It's possible that an angel told her, or perhaps because she was filled with the Holy Spirit she just sensed it. But she did know right away, and so did her child John.

Why were people surprised when Elizabeth said that the baby would be named John? There was no one named John in their family, and the people expected the baby to be named after his father.

What did their neighbors think of all this? All of the people throughout the hill country noticed that amazing things were happening: Elizabeth was pregnant at an old age, Zacharias was mute during the pregnancy, the child was named John and then Zacharias regained his speech. They knew a special baby had been born, and wondered who he would be.

Advanced Discussion Idea:

We have seen many stories where angels come to people to announce some important news. We have seen Sarah laugh, and we have seen Zacharias argue with the angel, and we have seen Joachim, Anna and Mary believe the angel without question. When Zacharias agreed to name their newborn son, John, he was immediately able to speak again. Now that he had seen the angel's words come true, and had done his part to give this name that the angel provided, His voice returned, so that he could glorify God.

Scripture references: *Luke 1: 39-80*

Righteous Joseph

*T*he *Lord* promised Abraham that his children would be like the stars: so many that they cannot be counted.

Abraham begot Isaac, and then Isaac begot Jacob, and Jacob begot Judah and his brothers. The Lord promised each of them that their children would become nations, and as Jacob told Judah, the scepter would stay with him – the King of Kings, the Son of God, would come through Judah's line.

Judah had a son named Perez, through Perez came his great-great-great-great grandson Salmon who begot Boaz by Rahab who protected Joshua's spies. Boaz begot Obed by Ruth who was loyal to Naomi and the One True God, and Obed begot Jesse who had many sons. Jesse begot David, who defeated Goliath and became a great king. David the king begot Solomon by the woman who had been the wife of his friend, Uriah. Solomon and his many children became a line of bad kings, and his great-great-great-great grandson was Uzziah, who was the king when the Prophet Isaiah saw the angels circling God's throne, and prophesied that a virgin would give birth to the Savior.

Uzziah's great-great-great grandson, Josiah begot Jeconiah about the time when the Israelites were carried away to Babylon; at that time, it was fourteen generations since King David. In Babylon, the family line continued, for fourteen more generations until finally Matthan begot Jacob, and Jacob begot Joseph the husband of Mary, of whom was born Jesus Christ.

And of course Joseph was married for forty years and had a wonderful family, but his wife died. Then one day the high priest Zacharias asked all of the widowed men to come and place their rod in the holiest of holies, to see who should take care of the young virgin who did not wish to marry. When Joseph's rod miraculously grew three leaves, everyone knew that God had chosen him to protect young Mary. So Mary was betrothed to Joseph, and then she was pregnant by the Holy Spirit.

Joseph had agreed to protect a young virgin; but if now she was pregnant, he thought she must not really want to live a chaste and holy life as she had said. Joseph could have humiliated her and asked for her to be punished. But he was a good man, and he did not want to make her a public example, so he was thinking that he would put her away secretly.

But while he thought about these things, an angel of the Lord appeared to him in a dream, saying, "Joseph, son of David, do not be afraid to take to you Mary your wife, for that which is conceived in her is of the Holy Spirit. And she will bring forth a Son, and you shall call His name Jesus, for He will save His people from their sins."

So all this was done that it might be fulfilled which was spoken by the Lord through the prophet, saying: "Behold, the virgin shall be with child, and bear a Son, and they shall call His name Immanuel," which means, "God with us."

Then Joseph, being aroused from sleep, did as the angel of the Lord commanded him and took to him his wife, and he called the baby Jesus.

Questions:

It is Joseph who is in the family of Abraham and King David, so it was important for him to be chosen to protect Mary, becoming her husband. Why do the Scriptures tell us about the genealogy of Jesus? Why does it matter that Joseph is born to this particular family line? The Scriptures explain the genealogy of Jesus Christ, so that we will understand that God fulfills his promise to Abraham and to all of the people along Abraham's line when he sends Jesus to them. For many generations He promised that the King of Kings would come through this family line, and God keeps His promises.

When Joseph learned that Mary was pregnant, he could have humiliated her and had her punished. Why didn't he? He was a good man and did not want to make an example of her, so he thought instead he would put her away quietly.

What did the angel explain to Joseph? He explained that Joseph did not need to put Mary away, because she was actually pregnant with God's own Son by the Holy Spirit. Instead, he should take her as his wife and name the baby Jesus.

Advanced Discussion Idea:

The genealogy of Jesus Christ runs from Abraham through David; along the way we find upstanding fathers like Abraham and Jacob, as well as the harlot Rahab from Jericho and the Moabite Ruth. The people of Israel are in this genealogy, and some outsiders through their love for God and His people show up in the family tree as well. This list finally leads to the King of Kings, Jesus Christ, through the righteous Joseph, who was very much the father and protector of our Lord, even though of course God was truly His Father.

Joseph was in a difficult position, because he did not hear from the angel until after he knew that Mary was pregnant, and yet even when he thought the worst, he would not consider humiliating Mary, but was merciful. In the icon of the Nativity we see him tormented by a demon, who is trying to make him doubt Mary's sincerity and the holiness of this birth. Joseph withstood these temptations, and steadfastly protected the Holy Virgin and the child Jesus throughout His youth.

Scripture references:
Matthew chapter 1

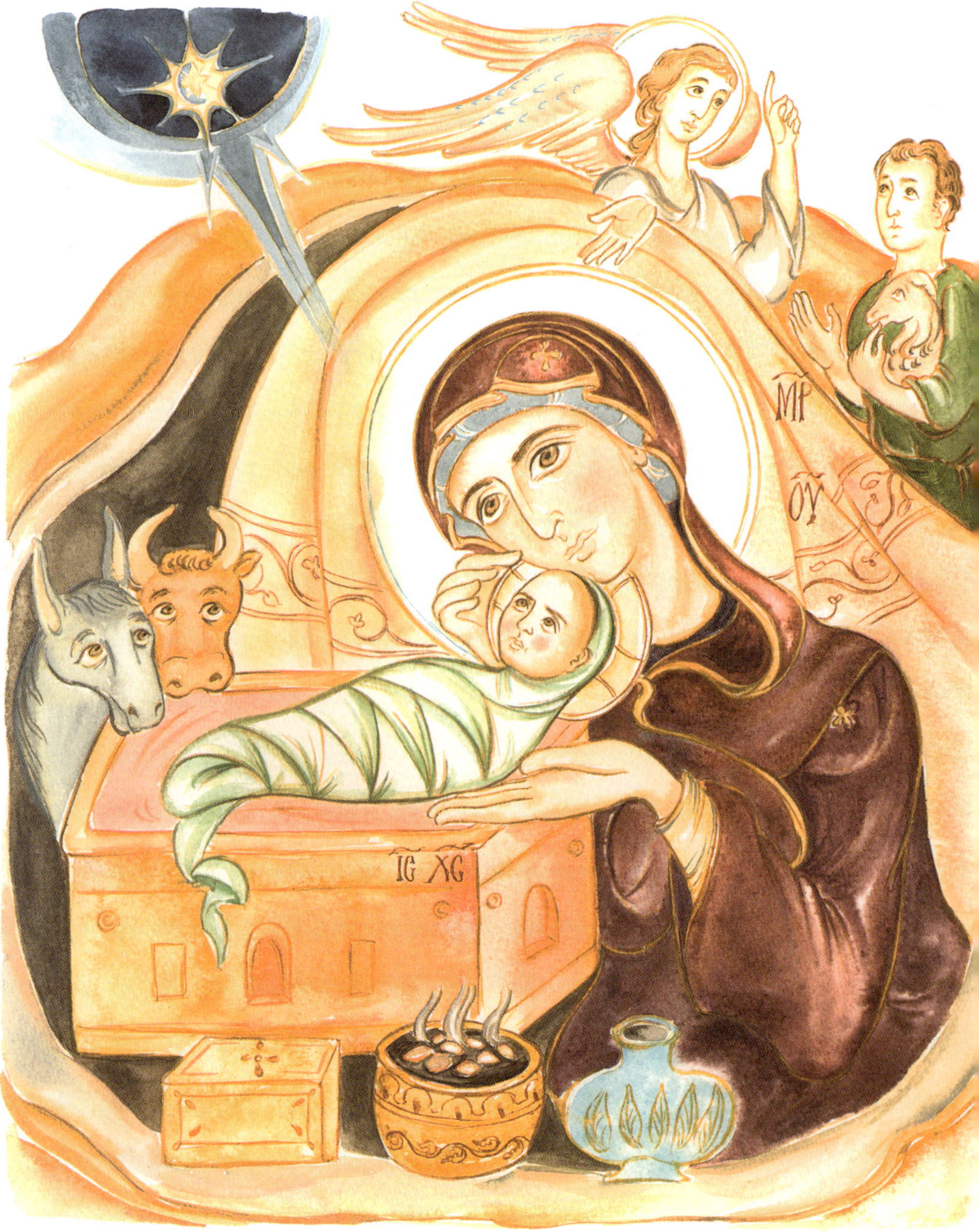
ΜΡ
ΘΥ
IC XC

A Child is Born in Bethlehem

And it came to pass in those days that a decree went out from Caesar Augustus that all the world should be registered, everyone in his own city. Joseph and Mary went up from Galilee, out of the city of Nazareth, into Judea, to the city of David, which is called Bethlehem, because he was of the house of David. While they were in Bethlehem, it was time for Mary's child to be born.

There was no room for them in any of the inns or buildings in town. They found a place among the animals, in a cave where the livestock was kept. Mary gave birth to the Son of God, and wrapped Him in swaddling cloths, and laid Him in a manger.

Now there were in the same country some shepherds living out in the fields, keeping watch over their flock by night. And behold, an angel of the Lord stood before them, and the glory of the Lord shone around them, and they were greatly afraid. But the angel said to them, "Do not be afraid, for behold, I bring you good tidings of great joy for all people. For there is born to you this day in the city of David a Savior, who is Christ the Lord. And this will be the sign to you: you will find a Babe wrapped in swaddling cloths, lying in a manger."

And suddenly there was were many more angels with this one, and they were all praising God and saying: "Glory to God in the highest, and on earth peace, goodwill toward men!"

When the angels had gone away from them into heaven, the shepherds said to one another, "Let us go to Bethlehem and see this thing that has come to pass, which the Lord has made known to us." And they hurried to Bethlehem and found Mary and Joseph, and the Babe lying in a manger.

Now when they had seen Him, they told everyone what the angel had said, and all those who heard it were amazed.

Mary kept all these things and pondered them in her heart.

Then the shepherds returned home, glorifying and praising God for all the things that they had heard and seen.

The magi were on their way to worship Him too! They had watched over the years until the star that the Prophet Daniel promised appeared, and then they followed it. The star moved with them on their journeys, until it stood right over the spot where the young Child was. When they saw the star, they rejoiced with exceedingly great joy. And when they came inside, they saw the young Child with Mary His mother, and fell down and worshiped Him. And when they had opened their treasures, they presented gifts to Him: gold, frankincense, and myrrh.

Christ is born! Glorify Him!

Questions:

Why did Joseph and Mary have to travel to Bethlehem? Caesar Augustus decreed that everyone must be registered in their own city, and because Joseph came from the line of David, they traveled to the city of David to be counted.

Why was Christ born in a manger? There was no room in the inn for the Holy Family, so they found a place among the livestock in a cave. When Christ was born, He was wrapped in swaddling cloths and laid in the manger.

Who told the shepherds that Christ was born? An angel of the Lord appeared to them and announced His birth, and then a multitude of angels came and sang praises to God.

How did the wise men or magi know where to find the newborn king? Daniel told them to follow the star when it came, and so they did. The star moved ahead of them and they followed, until it stood still right over the spot where Christ was.

Advanced Discussion Idea:

God can do anything, and He could have arranged for His own Son, the King of Kings, to be born in a palace but He did not; He chose for His Son to be born in a humble cave. Jesus did not come to earth to get rich — what money does God need? Jesus did not come to take the finest palace and sleep in the finest bed. He came to live in the humblest way, to share the most basic human experiences. Jesus would never own a home, but instead He would live like the poorest people and suffer alongside us through all of the indignities of our world. The first people called to worship him were poor and uneducated shepherds, because God does not care whether we are important to the world; every one of us is important in God's eyes, and our Lord has come for each and every one of us.

Scripture references:
Luke 2: 1-20, Matthew 2: 1-12

Published by
Sebastian Press
Western American Diocese of the Serbian Orthodox Church

Christian Inspiration for Youth Series, number 2

Prepress & printing
Interklima—grafika, Vrnjci, Serbia

Copyright © 2017 Sebastian Press

Address all correspondence to:
Sebastian Press
1621 West Garvey Avenue
Alhambra, California 91803
Email: info@westsrbdio.org
Website: www.westsrbdio.org

Publishers Cataloging in Publication

Names: Bjeletich, Elissa, author. | Jeftić, Jelena, illustrator.
Title: Welcoming the Christ child : family readings for the Nativity Lent / Elissa Bjeletich ; illustrated by Jelena Jeftić.

Description: Alhambra, California : Sebastian Press / Western American Diocese of the Serbian Orthodox Church, 2016. | Series: Christian inspiration for youth series ; no. 2.

Identifiers: ISBN: 9781936773305 | LCCN: 2016962994

Subjects: LCSH: Jesus Christ—Nativity—Orthodox Eastern Church. | Jesus Christ—Nativity—Prayers and devotions. | Jesus Christ—Nativity—Relation to the Old Testament. | Messiah—Prophecies. | Christmas—Orthodox Eastern Church. | Christmas—Prayers and devotions. | Epiphany season—Orthodox Eastern Church. | Bible—Prophecies. | Bible—Gospels—Relation to the Old Testament. | Orthodox Eastern Church—Doctrines.

Classification: LCC: BX376.35.N38 B54 2016 | DDC: 232.92—dc23